Decorating

with

Stencils

Innovative Designs

•

Step-by-Step
Instructions

•

Templates

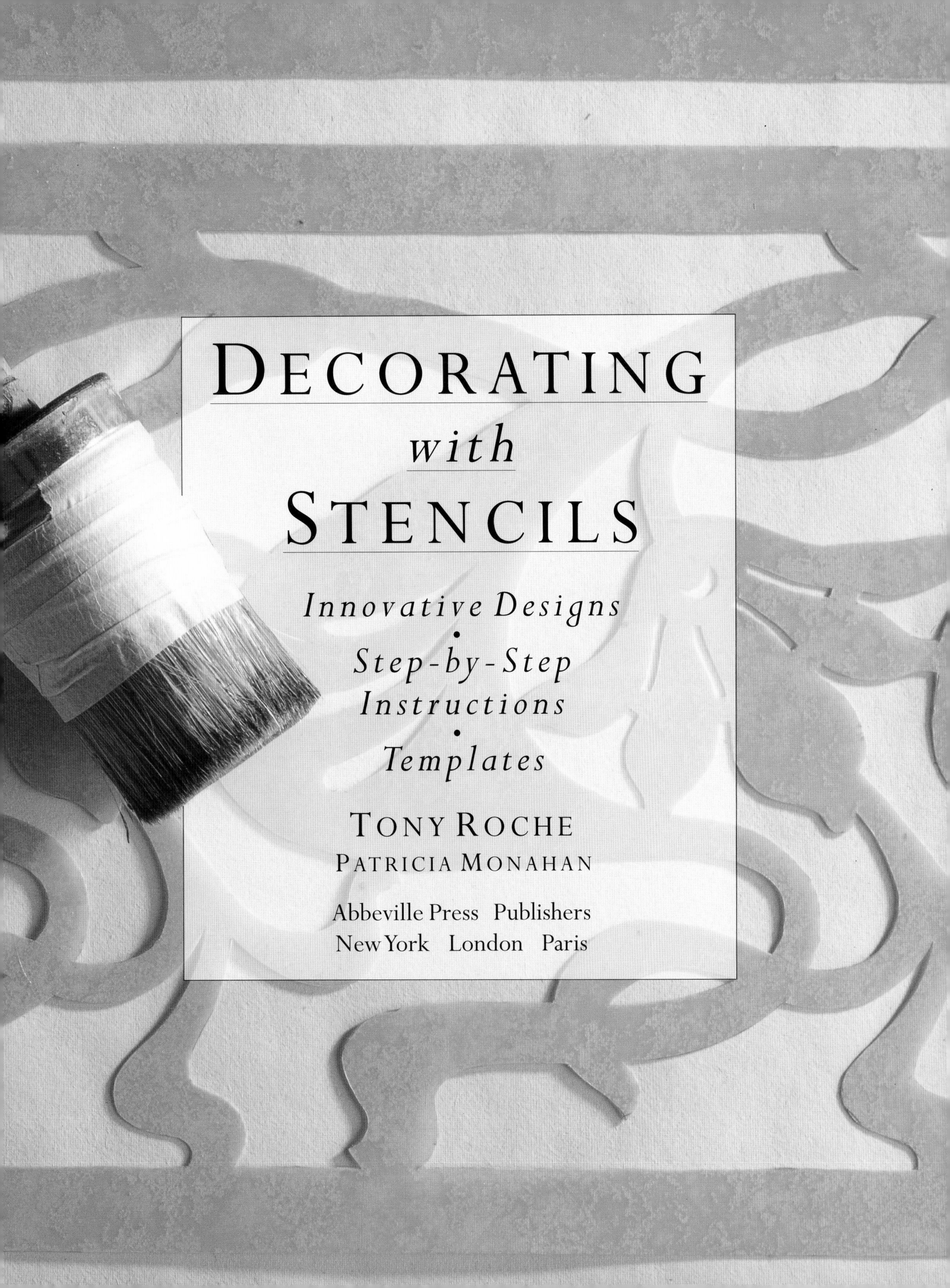

DECORATING
with
STENCILS

Innovative Designs
•
Step-by-Step
Instructions
•
Templates

TONY ROCHE
PATRICIA MONAHAN

Abbeville Press Publishers
New York London Paris

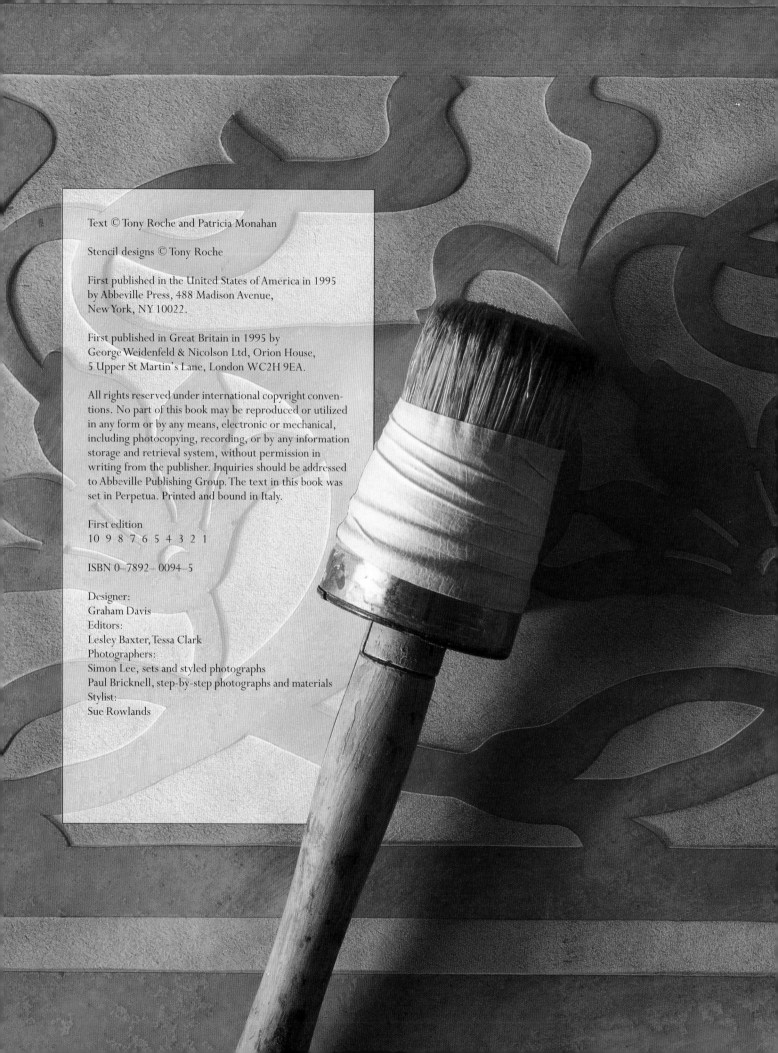

Designer:
Graham Davis
Editors:
Lesley Baxter, Tessa Clark
Photographers:
Simon Lee, sets and styled photographs
Paul Bricknell, step-by-step photographs and materials
Stylist:
Sue Rowlands

ACKNOWLEDGEMENTS

The authors and publishers would like to thank the following suppliers who lent properties and furniture for the sets in this book.

MOULDINGS, PICTURE RAILS AND SKIRTING BOARDS:
W.H. Newson,
481-491 Battersea Park Road,
London SW11 4NH

3: *Traditional Scandinavian Folk Art*
Table and chair:
Decorative Living,
55 New King's Road,
London SW6 4SE

4: *Simple 'Moderne' Style*
Picture and accessories:
Global Village,
249 Fulham Road,
London SW3 6HY

5: *High Victorian Gothic Design*
Antique doors:
The London Architectural Salvage and Supply Company Ltd,
Mark Street,
London EC2A 4ER

6: *Medieval Heraldic Style*
Floor lamp:
Designers Guild,
267 King's Road,
London SW3 5EN

FURNITURE:
The Furniture Union,
46 Beak Street,
London W1R 3DA

7: *Indian Paisley Motifs*
Furniture:
David Wainwright,
61/63 Portobello Road,
London W11 3DB

8: *Moroccan Tile Patterns*
Conservatory furniture and accessories:
Global Village,
249 Fulham Road,
London SW3 6HY

BATHROOM FITTINGS:
C.P. Hart and Sons Ltd,
212 Hercules Road,
London SE1 7LD

BATHROOM ACCESSORIES AND STOOL:
Global Village,
249 Fulham Road,
London SW3 6HY

9: *Modern Inspiration from Ancient Egypt*
Modern chair:
The Furniture Union,
46 Beak Street,
London W1R 3DA

10: *French Empire Style*
Footstool:
Mulberry,
11 Gees Court,
London W1M 5HQ

Handbasin and taps:
C.P. Hart and Sons Ltd,
212 Hercules Road,
London SE1 7LD

The authors and publishers would also like to thank Swann-Morton Limited for the scalpels and blades used throughout the book; Winsor & Newton for alkyd and oil paints; Liquitex for acrylic paints and texture gels.

The authors would also like to thank Simon Cobley for the patience with which he bore a year of disruption, Mary Fitzmaurice for her creative contribution and John Watson for help with set building.

Tony Roche would like to thank the BBC, in particular David Gray, for permitting him to work on this book. Others who have helped in a variety of ways are: Michael Connery, Christopher Nevile of 'The Study'; David Payton; Simon and Cornelia Playle; Alistair Merchant and Yvonne White.

CONTENTS

INTRODUCTION

Decorating with Stencils is unashamedly ambitious in its intentions and bold in its approach. It takes stencilling beyond the simple floral border and shows that this traditional technique can be used in a manner that is new, exciting and contemporary. The book provides clear step-by-step information for the beginner and ideas, projects and novel techniques which will inspire and delight the most experienced practitioner.

THE PLEASURES OF STENCILLING

Stencilling is a simple, enjoyable and practical method of applying ornamental detail to almost any surface. The combination of creativity and craftsmanship offers pleasures which can be enjoyed by everyone from skilled artists and professional decorators to those who consider themselves artistically inept. One of the joys of stencilling, and the quality which makes it so accessible, is its unique combination of control and freedom. The stencil plate imposes rigid boundaries within which you can apply paint freely and quickly. The plate is taped to the surface, paint is applied and then the stencil plate is peeled back to reveal the miraculously crisp and clearly defined painted pattern beneath.

Stencilling appeals to our innate love of repetition, symmetry and order.

Stencilling appeals to our innate love of repetition, symmetry and order. This sense of pattern can be seen in our enjoyment of decoration and ornamentation in the home and even on the clothes we wear. The stencil plate allows you to devise and apply your own designs, but without the uncertainty of freehand painting. But don't think of stencilling as simply a substitute for painting. It is a craft in its own right, capable of decorative effects which cannot be achieved in any other way –

and it is those possibilities which we want to present to you in this book.

Another appealing and surprising aspect of stencilling is the speed with which decoration can be applied to a surface – even when you are working on a large scale. Admittedly the preparatory stages of a complex stencil plate take time and concentration but once the stencil is cut the paint can be applied with surprising speed.

For the stenciller different kinds of enjoyment can be found in each stage of the process. Finding a pattern and translating it into a stencil design demands planning and application. Drawing and cutting requires manual dexterity and concentration. With each stencil that you cut, your movements become more confident and you handle the knife with more fluency. But the stencil is wonderfully forgiving so that slips of the knife and errors become incorporated in the pattern. Indeed an error repeated many times becomes less obvious than a single mistake, and can give a design an appealingly handmade charm.

THE USES OF STENCILLING

Stencils can be used on a small scale and sparingly or they can be a major component of a decorative scheme. They can ornament a plain object or introduce period detail or a splash of colour in an interior. They can even be used in an illusionistic way to replicate the appearance of another surface like tiles, wallpaper or stone. A few stencilled details can revive a tired decorative scheme or provide linking motifs so that disparate elements are pulled together to create a harmonious whole.

ABOUT THIS BOOK

The book divides into three main sections. In Chapters 1–2 the the reader is introduced to the materials and led step-by-step through all the processes from designing and manu-

facturing stencil plates to a description of the various systems for applying paint. All the main techniques are explained fully and clearly with an emphasis on practical applications. There is advice on avoiding problems where possible and solving them where it is necessary. You will be shown how to make a pattern work as a stencil, how to plan a decoration and how to deal with problems like taking a design around a corner. An invaluable aid to the novice, this first section will prove a useful reference for practitioners of all levels of ability.

Chapters 3–10 comprise the core of the book: 27 projects arranged in a series of eight room-sets based on period or regional themes. The sets have been carefully devised to show the incredible scope of stencil decoration, from the simple understated elegance of 'Moderne' to the flamboyance of the French Empire style. The projects too are diverse, from a Victorian all-over pattern which emulates wallpaper, to floor tiles and wall tiles, a variety of

borders and friezes, and decoration applied to smaller objects such as lampshades, boxes, trays and cushions. The book is peppered with practical hints, tips and tricks-of-the trade.

The techniques illustrated range from the simple and traditional to the ground-breaking. For example, texture compound is mixed with paint and used to replicate the appearance of beautiful (and costly) antique tiles. Acrylic texture mediums are used to enliven a simple motif. Oil paint is applied through a stencil to create the appearance of inlaid wood and a way of using lace to create a delightful all-over wall decoration is described. A traditional 'wipe-out' technique pioneered by W. W. Davidson in the 1920s allows you to introduce subtly gradated tones rather than the flat colour typical of most stencilled designs.

In the final section you will find the templates and all the information you need to create the stencils used in this book. Using these you can carry out the projects, re-creating some

Books old and new, prints, tiles, textiles and old wallpapers are just part of the rich vein of ready-made ornamentation and pattern waiting to be exploited by the stencil designer. It is also worth looking in second-hand bookshops for out-of-print books such as *Stencilling for Craftsmen* by the decorator-craftsman W. G. Sutherland. Published in the 1920s, it is a fund of sound advice and good designs. Here painted up patterns allow you to explore designs and colourways. They can then be translated into stencil designs

exactly, taking elements from others, selecting and modifying them to suit your own tastes and requirements. Once cut the stencil plate can be used time and time again, for by varying the colour and the method of application you will be able to create results which are remarkably different.

We hope that you will be so captivated by this satisfying and underestimated craft that you will begin to create your own designs.

SOURCES AND INSPIRATION

As you develop a stenciller's eye for pattern you will begin to see potential designs everywhere – in books, carved on to the facades of buildings, and embellishing furniture, tiles and household china. With practice you will become adept at translating these motifs into patterns that work as stencils.

Pattern can be divided into two broad categories: organic and geometric. From the earliest times nature has been plundered for the richly varied shapes of flowers and leaves, the sinuous curves of stems and tendrils and the simple forms of vegetables and fruits. Indeed, the simplest stencil in this book is a leaf drawn freehand, while a pineapple – a fruit with a delightfully strange appearance – has been used to create a stripe which has the boldness of traditional folk art.

Throughout the ages these naturally occurring forms have been stripped down and then simplified to emphasize their flat, pattern-making qualities so that they ultimately become almost abstract. This can be seen in the lily and lotus designs of ancient Egypt, the palmette, anthemion and honeysuckle motifs of ancient Greece and rhythmic scrolling arabesques to be found throughout the Muslim world. These patterns, refined over centuries, have a simple elegance and they are constantly revived and recycled, each age giving them a contemporary twist.

Geometric patterns also have a long history and have found especial favour this century.

In this book we show you how to construct the traditional Greek key or meander while a geometric lattice is applied to a cabinet and an abstract pattern of circles and curves is used for a traditional floorcloth.

It is easier to 'borrow' ready-made patterns than to try and evolve your own. Most patterns can be re-interpreted as stencil designs by adding ties to make the stencil plate self-supporting. These ties should be in keeping with the spirit and style of the pattern so that they become a part of it. You will find a rich source of material in specialist books on ornament from different periods and by different designers. But general interest magazines and travel books, wallpaper and fabrics are also rich sources. And for the stenciller, visits to museums, churches and historic houses can prove particularly rewarding.

As you develop a stenciller's eye for pattern you will begin to see potential designs everywhere ...

COLOUR

A stencilled pattern is created by applying colours over a base colour. The degree of contrast between the base colour and the applied colour will affect the way the pattern is perceived. Strong contrasts make the pattern stand out crisply against the background and are best for single motifs and for small details like borders. If, however, you use different tones of the same colour, the result will be a subtle self-coloured effect ideal for a restful all-over design. Slightly muted or 'dirtied' colours like terracotta and golden ochre are generally easier to work with than pure primaries which can be strident when used in large amounts. Spend time experimenting with colour combinations before you commit yourself.

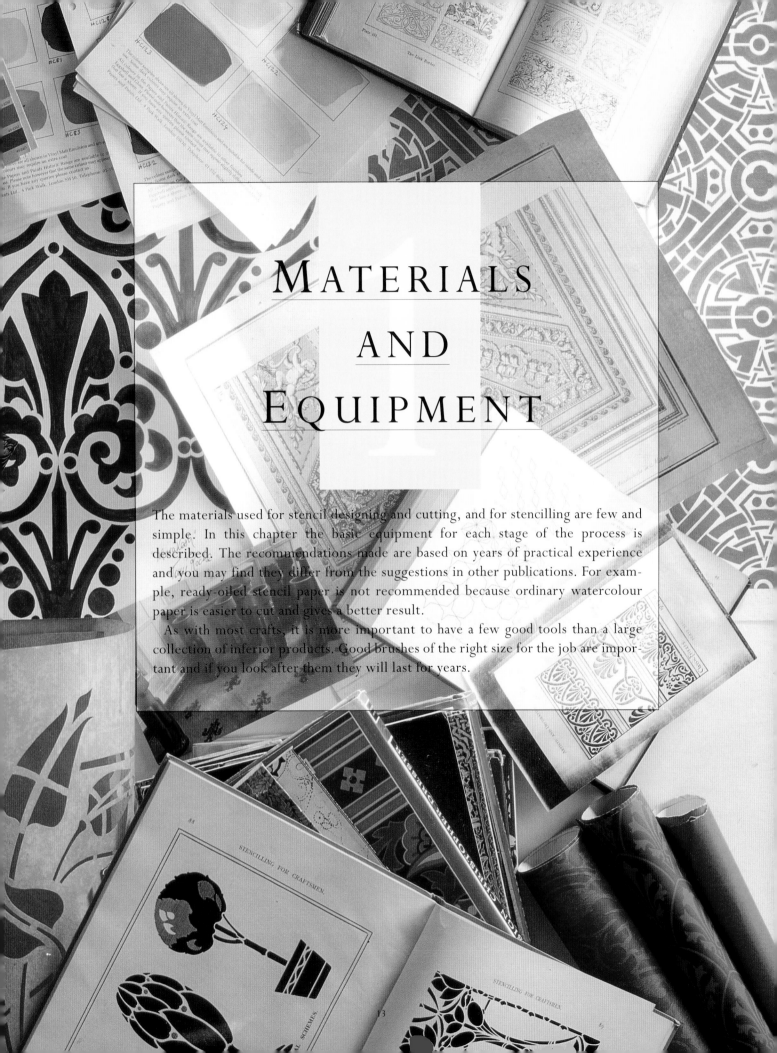

MATERIALS
AND
EQUIPMENT

The materials used for stencil designing and cutting, and for stencilling are few and simple. In this chapter the basic equipment for each stage of the process is described. The recommendations made are based on years of practical experience and you may find they differ from the suggestions in other publications. For example, ready-oiled stencil paper is not recommended because ordinary watercolour paper is easier to cut and gives a better result.

As with most crafts, it is more important to have a few good tools than a large collection of inferior products. Good brushes of the right size for the job are important and if you look after them they will last for years.

Oiled paper

Saunders
Waterford
356gsm

Arches 300gsm

Lining paper

14

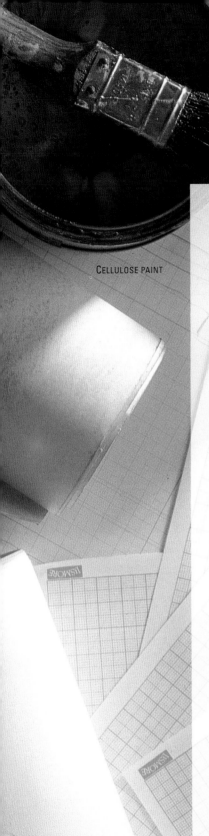

CELLULOSE PAINT

PAPERS

A pad of cheap cartridge will be useful for jotting down design and colour ideas, and for planning projects.

Gridded or sectional paper printed on one side with a grid of squares is used for drawing up templates. It is available as pads or sheets in a choice of metric or imperial rulings.

Stencils are cut from good quality watercolour paper which must have a smooth, hot pressed (HP) surface. Art and graphic supply shops will stock suitable papers as pads, single sheets and on the roll. Watercolour paper is available in a range of weights expressed as grams per square metre (gsm) or pound (lb) weight per 500 sheets. The weight you use will depend on the size of the stencil, the complexity of the cutting and the expected life of the stencil. For a detailed stencil which requires delicate cutting like the Pugin all-over pattern (page 70) you will need a light paper, say 220gsm (90lb). But you would use a heavier paper (300gsm/140lb) for the Moroccan tile design (page 94). When the stencil has been drawn, the paper is coated with linseed oil (light paper on one side, heavy paper on both sides) and hung up to dry. The oiled paper cuts beautifully. The finished stencil is painted or sprayed with a metallic cellulose paint such as Hammerite. This seals and protects it from paint. Clean the paint applicator with cellulose thinner.

Ready-oiled stencil paper is too heavily oiled and too thick for accurate cutting. Acetate is not recommended as cutting is difficult to control and it eventually becomes brittle and breaks.

A roll of lining paper is ideal for practising the stencilling techniques described on page 34 and also for exploring colour combinations.

FABRIANO 220GSM

LINSEED OIL

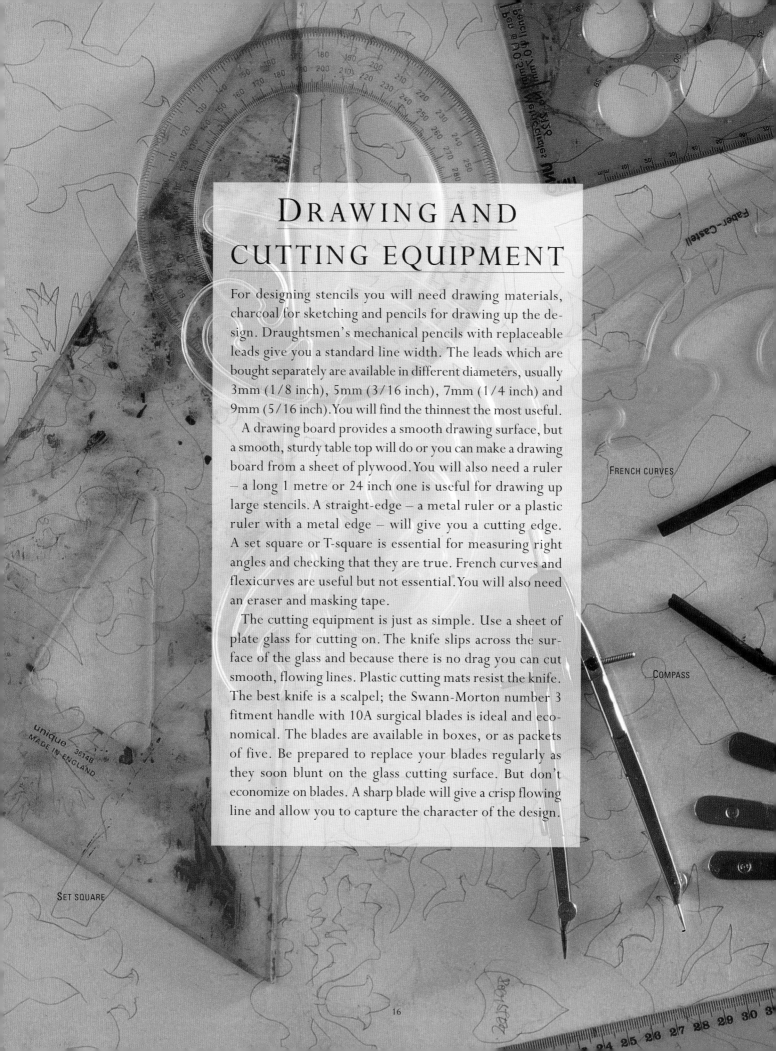

DRAWING AND CUTTING EQUIPMENT

For designing stencils you will need drawing materials, charcoal for sketching and pencils for drawing up the design. Draughtsmen's mechanical pencils with replaceable leads give you a standard line width. The leads which are bought separately are available in different diameters, usually 3mm (1/8 inch), 5mm (3/16 inch), 7mm (1/4 inch) and 9mm (5/16 inch). You will find the thinnest the most useful.

A drawing board provides a smooth drawing surface, but a smooth, sturdy table top will do or you can make a drawing board from a sheet of plywood. You will also need a ruler – a long 1 metre or 24 inch one is useful for drawing up large stencils. A straight-edge – a metal ruler or a plastic ruler with a metal edge – will give you a cutting edge. A set square or T-square is essential for measuring right angles and checking that they are true. French curves and flexicurves are useful but not essential. You will also need an eraser and masking tape.

The cutting equipment is just as simple. Use a sheet of plate glass for cutting on. The knife slips across the surface of the glass and because there is no drag you can cut smooth, flowing lines. Plastic cutting mats resist the knife. The best knife is a scalpel; the Swann-Morton number 3 fitment handle with 10A surgical blades is ideal and economical. The blades are available in boxes, or as packets of five. Be prepared to replace your blades regularly as they soon blunt on the glass cutting surface. But don't economize on blades. A sharp blade will give a crisp flowing line and allow you to capture the character of the design.

FRENCH CURVES

COMPASS

SET SQUARE

CIRCLE TEMPLATE

MASKING TAPE

FLEXICURVE

CHARCOAL

MECHANICAL PENCILS
AND LEADS

SCALPEL AND BLADES

17

STIPPLER TAPED
TO TIGHTEN THE
BRISTLES

NATURAL SPONGE

STENCILLING BRUSHES

WHISTLER STIPPLER

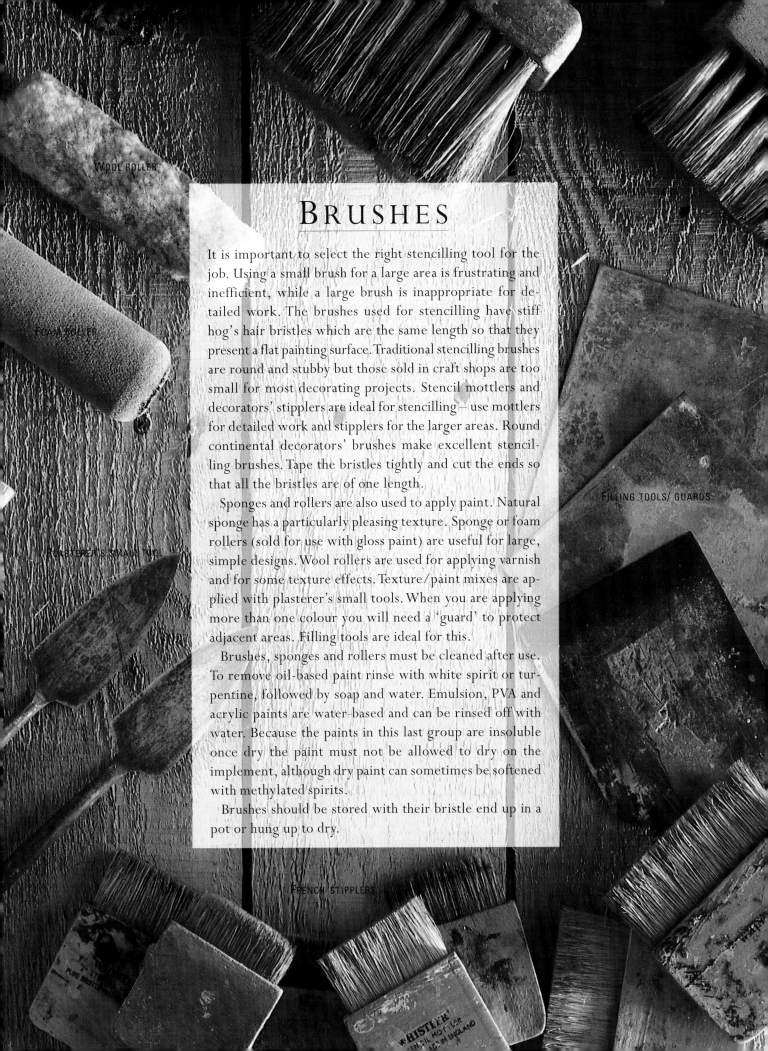

BRUSHES

It is important to select the right stencilling tool for the job. Using a small brush for a large area is frustrating and inefficient, while a large brush is inappropriate for detailed work. The brushes used for stencilling have stiff hog's hair bristles which are the same length so that they present a flat painting surface. Traditional stencilling brushes are round and stubby but those sold in craft shops are too small for most decorating projects. Stencil mottlers and decorators' stipplers are ideal for stencilling – use mottlers for detailed work and stipplers for the larger areas. Round continental decorators' brushes make excellent stencilling brushes. Tape the bristles tightly and cut the ends so that all the bristles are of one length.

Sponges and rollers are also used to apply paint. Natural sponge has a particularly pleasing texture. Sponge or foam rollers (sold for use with gloss paint) are useful for large, simple designs. Wool rollers are used for applying varnish and for some texture effects. Texture/paint mixes are applied with plasterer's small tools. When you are applying more than one colour you will need a 'guard' to protect adjacent areas. Filling tools are ideal for this.

Brushes, sponges and rollers must be cleaned after use. To remove oil-based paint rinse with white spirit or turpentine, followed by soap and water. Emulsion, PVA and acrylic paints are water-based and can be rinsed off with water. Because the paints in this last group are insoluble once dry the paint must not be allowed to dry on the implement, although dry paint can sometimes be softened with methylated spirits.

Brushes should be stored with their bristle end up in a pot or hung up to dry.

WOOL ROLLER

FOAM ROLLER

PLASTERER'S SMALL TOOL

FILLING TOOLS/ GUARDS

FRENCH STIPPLERS

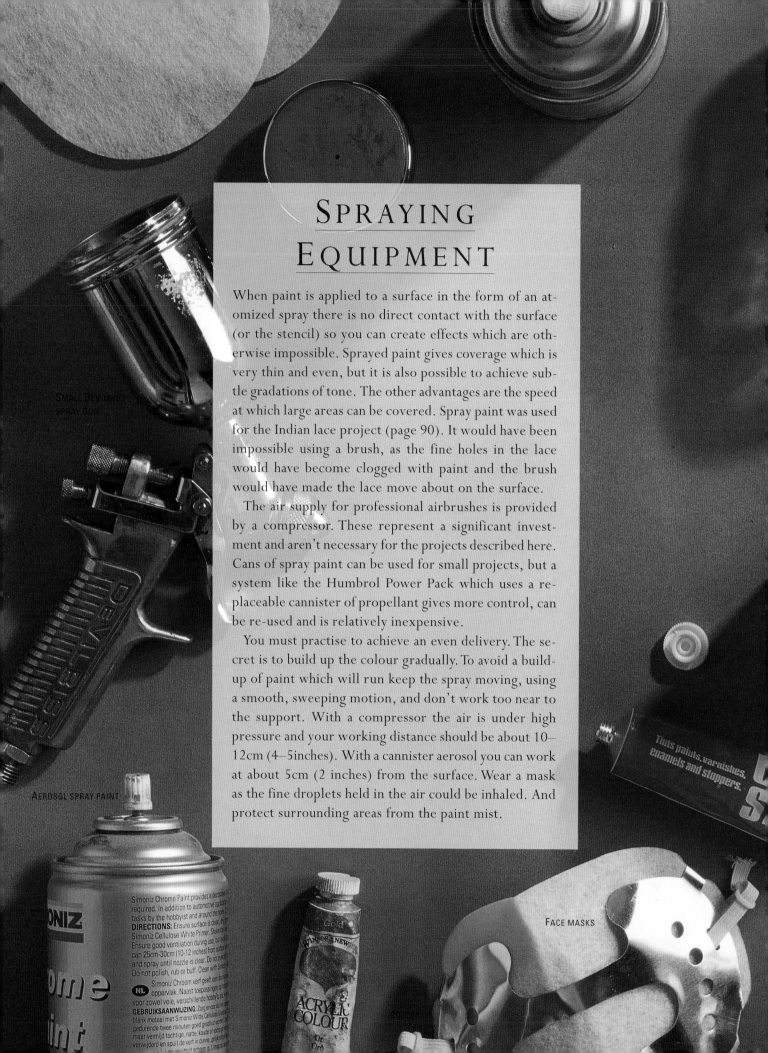

SPRAYING EQUIPMENT

When paint is applied to a surface in the form of an atomized spray there is no direct contact with the surface (or the stencil) so you can create effects which are otherwise impossible. Sprayed paint gives coverage which is very thin and even, but it is also possible to achieve subtle gradations of tone. The other advantages are the speed at which large areas can be covered. Spray paint was used for the Indian lace project (page 90). It would have been impossible using a brush, as the fine holes in the lace would have become clogged with paint and the brush would have made the lace move about on the surface.

The air supply for professional airbrushes is provided by a compressor. These represent a significant investment and aren't necessary for the projects described here. Cans of spray paint can be used for small projects, but a system like the Humbrol Power Pack which uses a replaceable cannister of propellant gives more control, can be re-used and is relatively inexpensive.

You must practise to achieve an even delivery. The secret is to build up the colour gradually. To avoid a build-up of paint which will run keep the spray moving, using a smooth, sweeping motion, and don't work too near to the support. With a compressor the air is under high pressure and your working distance should be about 10–12cm (4–5inches). With a cannister aerosol you can work at about 5cm (2 inches) from the surface. Wear a mask as the fine droplets held in the air could be inhaled. And protect surrounding areas from the paint mist.

SMALL DEVILBISS SPRAY GUN

AEROSOL SPRAY PAINT

FACE MASKS

Humbrol Power Pack

Large DeVilbiss spray gun

Small Badger airbrush

FABRIC PAINTS

OIL PAINTS

GOUACHE

EMULSION PAINT

PAINTS

There are two main types of paint: oil-based paints and water-based paints. Oil paints are tough and durable, but they are slow drying and must be thinned with white spirit or turpentine. They have been used for only one project in this book – the 'inlaid' effect on the 'Moderne' cabinet (page 56) was created using alkyd paints, a fast-drying form of traditional artists' oils.

Most of the other projects have been carried out in household emulsion paint, an emulsion of polyvinyl acetate (PVA) or acrylic polymer resins in which the pigment is held in suspension. Emulsion paint can be thinned with water but forms an insoluble film when dry. It dries rapidly, so waiting time is minimized and one layer can be applied over another very quickly. However, brushes and stencils must be rinsed as you go because the dry paint cannot be removed with water. Dry emulsion paint can be softened with methylated spirits, but the results are not always satisfactory so it is best not to let the paint dry on brushes, rollers or stencils.

You can tint emulsion paint with artists' acrylic or gouache. Oil paint can be tinted with artists' oil. Universal stainers can be used with water-based and oil paints.

Fabric paints are actually dyes in paint form. Once dry they are fixed by placing the fabric under a clean sheet of paper and ironing it.

Gold paint for the box on page 79 and the tray on page 68 was made from button polish (a shellac lacquer) and gold powder. The powder can be mixed with other mediums. You can also buy metallic gold paints. Paint applicators are cleaned with methylated spirits.

ACRYLIC TEXTURE PASTE

ALKYD

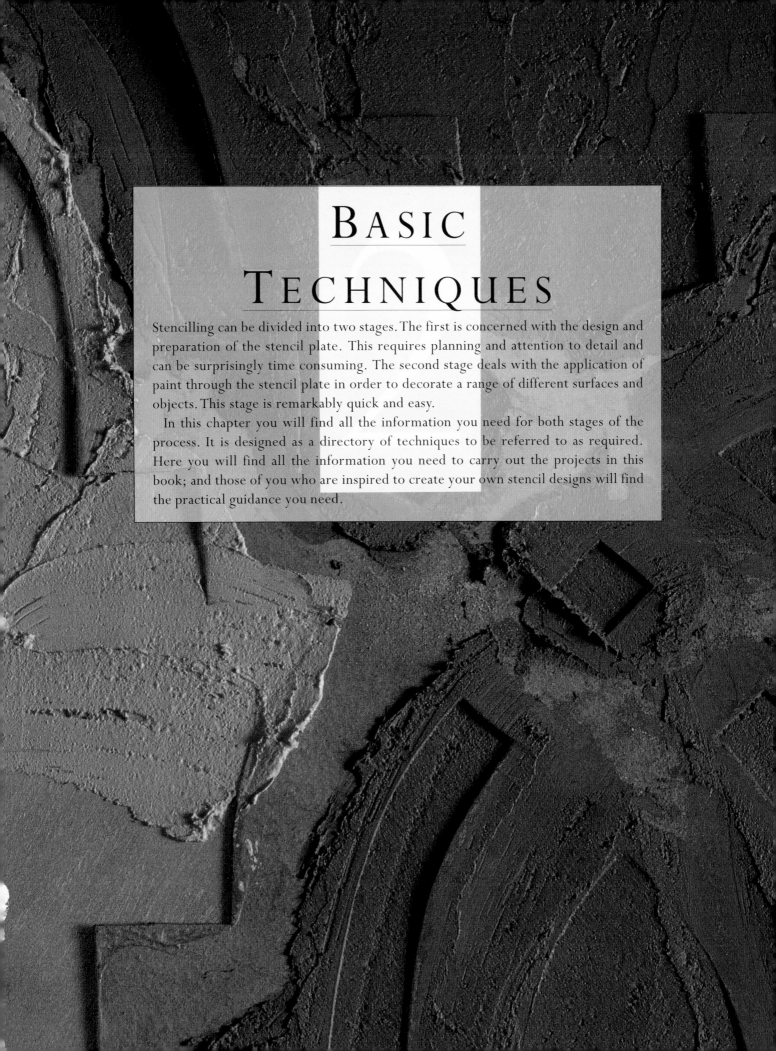

BASIC
TECHNIQUES

Stencilling can be divided into two stages. The first is concerned with the design and preparation of the stencil plate. This requires planning and attention to detail and can be surprisingly time consuming. The second stage deals with the application of paint through the stencil plate in order to decorate a range of different surfaces and objects. This stage is remarkably quick and easy.

In this chapter you will find all the information you need for both stages of the process. It is designed as a directory of techniques to be referred to as required. Here you will find all the information you need to carry out the projects in this book; and those of you who are inspired to create your own stencil designs will find the practical guidance you need.

HOW STENCILS WORK

There are four stages in the production of a stencilled decoration. These are: (1) *The original pattern* on which the stencil will be based.

(2) *The template.* The original pattern is translated into a template using one of the systems overleaf. The template is the smallest unit to which the pattern can be reduced and from which the stencil can be created.

(3) *The stencil plate.* This is really a complex mask. The stencil plate masks or protects those parts of the pattern which are not going to be painted. In a 'positive' stencil the background or 'negative' of the pattern is masked. In a 'negative' stencil the 'positive', the pattern itself, is masked so that the background of the ornament can be painted.

(4) *The stencilled decoration* is created by laying the stencil plate (mask) over the surface and applying paint through it.

The difficult part of the process is translating the original pattern (1) into the template (2) so that the stencil plate (3) works as a single unit and doesn't fall apart.

In a 'positive' stencil the plate represents the background or the 'negative' of the pattern. This isn't a single, continuous element, so if you traced a pattern on to paper and then cut it out it would fall apart. To transform these separate scraps of paper into a single, coherent stencil plate you need to tie them together. On a stencil plate these linkages are provided by 'ties' which form bridges between one part of the stencil and another.

The art of stencil design and cutting lies in the proper design and arrangement of the ties. The only way of really learning how to arrange them is to practise cutting templates and stencils. There is no substitute for experience and no better way of learning than to have a plate fall to pieces. Only then will you really begin to 'think in stencils'.

1 The original pattern
A pattern has been drawn and painted up as a source for a stencil design.

2 The template
The template comprises half the basic trefoil motif, plus half of the linking 'stalk' motif. By flopping this you complete the motif and by repeating it several times you build the pattern.

3 The stencil plate
To create the stencil plate the template has been traced, then flopped and traced. This has been repeated seven times.

4 The stencilled decoration
The wall has been stencilled with two repeats of the stencil plate.

Sometimes the ties hold the design together but the resulting stencil plate is too frail and will break when used. This problem can be overcome by interpreting the design so as to produce two stencil plates rather than one. If you look at the *Moroccan Tiled Wall* (page 94) and the *Dado with a Zig-Zag Motif* (page 110) you will find that two plates have been cut in order to produce stronger stencils.

Ties must perform the practical function of holding the stencil plate together, but that isn't enough. They must also be arranged so as to enhance and become part of the design. Suppose you had a flowing foliate border design based on vines, vine leaves and grapes it would be entirely inappropriate if the stencil plate was bristling with thick, stubby ties. Such a design demands delicate, flowing ones which are in sympathy with the organic character of the pattern. Equally, a crisp, geometric pattern should have crisp geometric ties. A sensitivity to the nature of the pattern will be necessary when you are cutting stencil plates from the templates provided in this book. Stencil cutting is just as creative and personal as drawing – in many ways you can think of it as drawing with a blade.

Stencil ties
The pattern above looks like a stencil design, but if it were cut it would fall apart.

In the centre pattern ties have been added but although they hold the plate together they are not in keeping with the design.

On the far right you can see that the ties are more sensitively handled. The flowing lines reflect, and have become part of, the design.

Positive
This shows a pattern applied through a 'positive' stencil plate. The plate masks the background so that paint is applied to the pattern area.

Negative
In this case the background has been painted using a 'negative' stencil plate. The stencil plate protected the pattern area from the paint.

On the right you can see see a template which has been correctly designed. On the far right the same template has fallen apart because there weren't enough ties to hold it together.

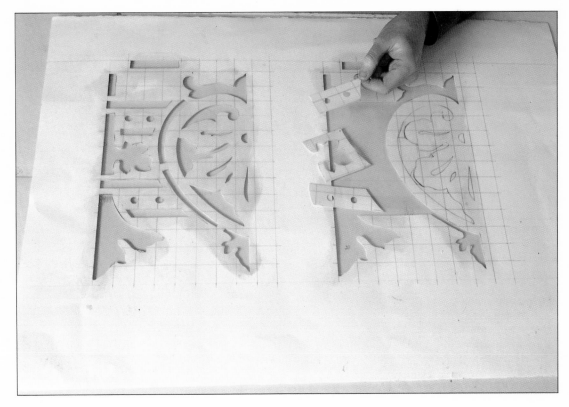

DRAWING AND CUTTING
THE TEMPLATE

You Will Need

●

Gridding up
Acetate, T-square or
set square, technical
pen size 0.1 or 0.2
Metric or imperial
gridded card
Masking tape, sheet of
plate glass and sharp
knife

Tracing the design
Original design, tracing
paper, pencil
Masking tape, sheet of
plate glass and sharp
knife

Using photocopies
Original design,
photocopy,
watercolour paper
Masking tape, sheet of
plate glass, sharp knife

●

The template is the key to a successful stencil. It is the smallest repeatable unit to which the stencil can be reduced. Templates are small and easy to store and should be filed away once you've drawn the stencil. If the stencil is damaged you can re-create it from the template – with a complex design this is much easier than re-creating the template. Avoid using the template as a stencil except in very special circumstances – on page 41 we show the template used to create a neat stop at a corner.

If the stencil is a single, non-repeating motif a template may not be necessary. On this page a photocopy is used to create a simple stencil, and the stencil for the floorcloth on page 60 was produced directly by gridding up from a piece of glass.

There are many methods of creating a template and the system you use will depend on the nature of your source or reference.

Gridding up. This technique involves drawing a grid on to an original image and then transferring the image square by square on to a second grid. The second grid may be larger, smaller or the same size. The grid may be drawn directly on to the original or, if the original is precious or difficult to draw on, you can draw a grid on a sheet of acetate and lay that over the drawing. To draw the grid on the acetate you will need a T-square or a set square and a fine permanent marker.

Next decide how big the template should be. If you want it twice as big, the squares on the sheet of paper will be twice the size of those on the original. Use a sheet of ready-gridded card and emphasize the relevant lines in pencil. So if the original consists of 15 x 15 2.5cm (1 inch) squares the final template drawing should be divided into 15 x 15 5cm (2 inch) squares.

Now reproduce the original square by square.

Gridding up
Lay a sheet of gridded acetate over the original. Identify the area which will give you the template. Here acetate with a grid of 1cm (3/8 inch) squares is laid over a book of ornament. The template was to be four times bigger than the original, so the grid was made up of 4cm (1 1/2 inch) squares. The drawing was transferred square by square on to the gridded paper, the contents of a 1cm (3/8 inch) square being re-created in a 4cm (1 1/2 inch) square.
On page 30 this template is used to create a border stencil. On pages 34—37 the stencil is painted up using several different techniques and applied to a wall.

You may find a system of numbered coordinates useful – like those on a map. Number the squares across the top of both grids then label the squares alphabetically down the vertical axis. Doing this will give every square on the grid a unique designation.

When the template has been drawn up and you are satisfied that the ties work, you can cut it out. Work on a sheet of plate glass and use a scalpel.

Tracing the design. A direct tracing is used when you want to produce a template which is the same size as the original. Lay the tracing paper over the original and trace off the outlines using a technical pencil. When you have completed the drawing remove the trace and lay it on to a sheet of gridded card, fixing it with masking tape. Lay the card and the trace on to a sheet of plate glass and, using a sharp knife, cut through both the trace and the card.

Using photocopies. A photocopier is a useful way of copying or enlarging an image. Enlarging with a photocopier is less flexible than gridding up because the increments available are limited. This is a simple way of enlarging the templates at the end of the book.

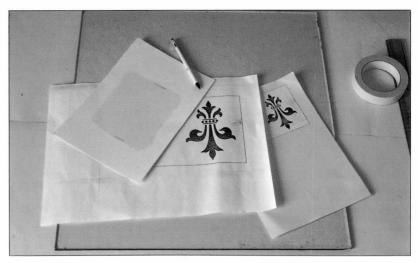

Using photocopies

Photocopies can be used to enlarge a stencil design and produce a stencil plate, avoiding the template stage.
Above: This shows the original image on the right, the enlarged photocopy and a sheet of oiled paper.
Right: The oiled paper is placed on a sheet of plate glass. The copy is taped to it and using a sharp knife the stencil is cut.

Tracing the design
Above: Lay tracing paper over the original design. Draw a vertical through the centre of the motif. Using a 0.1 or 0.2 technical pencil trace the design carefully.
Right: Place a sheet of gridded card on plate glass. Lay the trace over it, carefully aligning the vertical against the grid. Tape the trace firmly with masking tape. With a sharp knife cut through both the trace and the gridded paper. This is a simple and direct method of producing a template or simple stencil.

DRAWING THE STENCIL

Once the template is prepared you can use it to construct the stencil. Drawing a stencil isn't difficult, but you must plan if you are to avoid mistakes. Each stencil design poses different problems. A single motif such as that used to create the border around the lampshade on page 67 is so simple that you can draw and cut the stencil directly without an intervening template stage. The Pugin all-over pattern on page 71 is more complicated. First you must decide how many repeats there should be on the stencil plate – the bigger the plate the more cutting you have to do, but the faster the stencilling process will be. However, if the stencil plate is too big it will be unwieldy. You must also ensure that there are enough motifs to allow you to register repeats.

This isn't a problem with the Pugin design where the motifs are relatively small, but it could be with the Moroccan tile design on page 95 or the medieval wall hanging on page 83 in which the motifs are big.

A sketch of the way the template builds up into the stencil is useful. The design illustrated here requires four moves of the template. First the template is located to the left of the centre line, then it is flopped over on the centre line, creating a mirror image of the first motif. Then a part of the template is added at either end to create a link so that the design works as a continuous border. If you study the stencil carefully you will see that if the stencil didn't have these end motifs you would have to register each move against a straight line. It is difficult to register on a straight line and part of the background may show through at the junction. The foliate motif can be overlapped providing a solid register (see page 38).

This design provides its own register but many stencil designs need to have register marks incorporated. This is discussed on page 132.

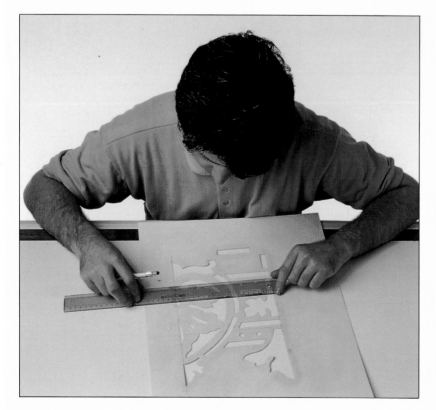

1 Fix a sheet of watercolour paper to the work surface. Draw a base line using a ruler. Tape a straight-edge below the base line and align the set square against it. Plot the centre of the stencil and its width. Measure the main construction points of the template and plot these on the stencil.

2 Using a set square draw verticals from the points plotted on the base line. Butt the set square against the straight-edge to ensure that the verticals are at right angles to the base line. These verticals will give you locations for the template.

3 Lay the template on the paper, aligning it against the centre line and the base line for the first move.

4 Fix the template to the paper with masking tape – it is important that it does not shift as you are drawing. Trace off one side of the template in pencil.

5 Turn the stencil over so that you can create the other half of the motif. Here the left side of the stencil was drawn first. The template was then flopped, and aligned on the centre and base lines. The mirror image was traced off to create the right side of the motif.

6 You now have one complete motif. To provide a link for the repeat you need to add a bit on to each end of the motif. Here you can see the template has been aligned on the drawing in order to complete the foliate motif. The parts of the template not being traced have been masked for clarity.

Cutting the Stencil

You Will Need

•

A dish of boiled
linseed oil
Cartridge paper
Straight-edge
A small decorator's
brush, rag, white spirit
or turpentine to clean
the brush
A sheet of plate glass,
a craft knife with a
good supply of blades.
A Swann-Morton no 3
fitment handle and
number 10A surgical
blades have been used
throughout this book.

•

Good stencil design depends on inspired cutting. When you are proficient you will be able to design with the knife, using the blade to put details and flourishes into a rough drawing. But as a beginner you need a meticulous drawing. If the stencil design is intricate you should block it in with paint, pencil or marker so that it is easier to 'see' the design and the areas which are to be cut away.

When the stencil has been drawn the paper should be brushed with boiled linseed oil and left to dry. Lighter weight papers need to be oiled on one side only, heavy papers (300gsm/ 140lb and over) should be oiled on both sides and hung up to dry. The oil makes the paper easier to cut, though paper that has been over-oiled is liable to become brittle.

You should cut on a sheet of toughened or plate glass because the knife glides across the surface without dragging. Glass is hard on blades, which have to be replaced frequently, but the crispness of the cut and the flowing quality of the line make the expense worthwhile. Make sure the glass is clear of scraps of paper and masking tape as these would impede the flow of the knife.

If this is your first stencil you should practise your cutting skills on scrap paper. Hold the knife like a pen and practise cutting straight lines against a ruler, using the tip of a sharp blade and steady pressure. Then try cutting curves, circles and sinuous lines. For big curves use a steady, sweeping gesture working from your shoulder, for smaller curves use your little finger as a pivot. Don't worry if your circles go out of true, or the knife slips here and there. The repeating nature of stencils means that minor irregularities are incorporated in the design and even add an individual charm. If a stencil is absolutely perfect it will look mechanical.

1 Stencil paper is treated with linseed oil to make it easier to cut. Pour some boiled linseed oil into a dish and apply it to one side of the cartridge paper with a bristle brush. One coat of oil will be enough – if the paper is over-oiled it will become brittle. (Bought stencil papers are often over-oiled and too thick.) Wipe off excess oil with a rag and leave the stencil to dry for 24 hours. To clean the brush wipe it on a rag, rinse it in white spirit or turpentine, wipe it again and then wash it in soapy water. Leave to dry in a jar, bristle end up.

2 Lay the drawn-up stencil on a sheet of glass. Always cut on glass and use a sharp knife. For most cutting you should hold the knife like a pen, gripping it firmly – but not too tightly or you will get cramp. Work freely, pivoting from the shoulder rather than the wrist and cut towards yourself. Here a straight-edge is being used as a guide for a straight line.

3 Here a curving line is being cut using the little finger as a pivot. The cutting process should not be rushed. The best cutting is done when you use the knife as a drawing tool, feeling your way around the outline of the motif, creating a line which captures the character of the particular design. Don't worry if there are flaws – nicks and slips of the blade will become incorporated in the stencilled pattern and give it an individual charm. When the stencil is cut it should be sealed with a protective material such as cellulose paint, see page 42.

APPLYING PAINT

You Will Need

●

Emulsion paint
Masking tape
A stencil plate
A piece of board to be
used as a palette
Lining paper to
practise on
The appropriate paint
applicator

●

Stencilling is surprisingly quick and easy once you have cut and prepared the stencil and there is immense satisfaction when you have applied the paint and peel back the plate to reveal the crisp, clean edges of the stencilled pattern.

Paint can be applied with a brush, a roller, a paint sprayer or a sponge using a variety of techniques. The technique you choose will depend on the type and size of the stencil, the area to be covered and the effect you want to achieve.

There are a few simple rules which apply whatever technique you use. The paint must be the right consistency – too thin and it will run, too heavy and it will clog the applicator. Most commercially available paints are of the correct consistency in the pot, but experiment before you start working on a project.

Be aware that factors like room temperature and the nature of your working surface will affect how the paint takes to the surface.

Don't dip the paint applicator into the paint pot – pour the paint, a bit at a time, into a paint tray or, better still, make yourself a palette from a bit of scrap board. Working from a palette gives you more control. You can see if the consistency and coverage is right, and knock off excess paint if necessary. A palette is lighter and easier to handle than a paint pot and using one also keeps the main paint supply clean.

The paint applicator must not be overloaded. If there is too much paint on the brush, roller or sponge the colour will seep under the stencil creating messy edges. Check that the applicator is correctly loaded each time you pick up more paint. If you are working with a stencilling brush, for example, start by dipping the tip of the bristles in the paint. Then work the brush over the palette using a tapping gesture. You will immediately be able to tell if

Stippling

You will need a round stencilling brush, a stencil mottler or a stippler for this technique. The bristles of these brushes are the same length so that they present a flat painting surface (see page 18). If the bristles on a round stencilling brush are long they can be stiffened by binding them tightly with PVC at the top, near the ferrule.
1 Dip the tip of the stippling brush in the paint. Now tap or pounce the brush on the palette. This removes excess paint from the brush, ensures that the paint is evenly distributed and allows you to check the effect. Don't overload the brush.

there is too much – or too little – paint on the brush.

Start by practising on lining paper. Fix the stencil to the paper using masking tape. If the stencil is large it may bulge away from the surface, especially if you are working on a vertical support such as a wall. To ensure that the paint doesn't seep under the stencil hold it close to the surface you are working on with your non-painting hand.

As you can see from the examples on the following pages, you can achieve very different results by varying the method of paint application. Experiment before you start a project and select the technique which is most appropriate. Stippling, the most versatile method of applying paint through a stencil, can be used for small intricate stencil designs as well as big, bold patterns. It is important to use a brush which is the right size for the job. If you use a small brush for a large stencil the colour will build up with frustrating slowness. But you need a small brush to get into the nooks and crannies of a delicately cut stencil. Sponge or foam rollers on the other hand are ideal for applying large areas of flat colour through a fairly open stencil design.

The stippled motif Stippling is the most popular and useful stencilling technique, and the easiest for the beginner to master. It is flexible, easily controlled and gives even coverage and a neat edge. You can lay a thin film of paint, build up intense colour or create modulated tones by varying the intensity of colour from one area to another.

2 Apply paint by tapping the brush on to the surface with a brisk, regular motion. Keeping the tip of the brush parallel to the surface, work over the entire exposed area, building up an even film of paint. You can increase the intensity of the paint colour and coverage by going over the area until you have achieved the tone you require – you'll be surprised by the smooth way the paint layer builds up. After a while the technique imposes a rhythm of its own.

Two-tone effect with stippling brush

In this variation on stippling two colours are applied, one over the other, to achieve subtle gradations of tone. Place a small pool of each colour on the palette. Stipple on a thin layer of the first colour. Change to a new brush and pick up the second colour. Stipple the second colour around the edges of the stencil apertures to create an almost sculptural effect.

Sponging

Dip a damp, natural sponge in a pool of paint. Knock the paint out on the palette and apply the sponge to the surface with a tapping motion. Work from side to side, building up the colour to the density you require. A thin paint application gives an open, speckled texture, which gradually fills in with each pass of the sponge. A densely sponged surface has a distinctive velvety bloom.

Paint roller

A sponge or foam roller provides a quick method of applying paint to a big area. It is most suited to simple, open designs. Pick up a little paint, being careful not to overload the roller. Work the roller across the palette to spread the paint. Apply the roller to the surface, working in different directions to get even coverage. Don't press on the roller or the paint will squelch out.

Brushing

Brushing allows paint to build up around the margins of the apertures giving the finished decoration a crisply defined look. Load a stiff bristle brush by dipping the tip into the paint on the palette. The paint is applied with a regular brushing action, constantly changing direction. Check coverage and consistency on the palette first – it should cover thinly, without dribbling.

Spraying

Spraying is ideal for large projects and delicate designs. It gives even coverage and neat, crisp edges. However, the result can be bit mechanical. Cover adjacent areas and wear a mask. Apply the paint with a regular, side to side, sweeping motion, allowing the paint film to build up gradually. The paint should be thinner than for other techniques; we recommend a 50:50 mix of paint and water.

Variegated effect with a roller

By applying two colours at once you can achieve a subtly variegated effect. Lay out both colours on the palette. Pick up a little of each colour on the roller and roll it out. The colours will begin to blend. Apply the loaded roller to the stencil using multi-directional movements. Don't press on the roller. The colours blend with a pleasing unpredictability.

APPLYING THE STENCIL TO A SURFACE

The project here shows how a simple, one-colour border stencil is applied as a frieze to a wall. The template is on page 132, and you'll find instructions for drawing and cutting the stencil on page 32. This project is used to make some general points.

With a stencil that involves repeats you must decide where to start and in what direction to proceed. Here we have centred the end design on the corner and worked the stencil from that point. You could start in the centre of the wall facing you or design a 'stop' to meet the corner (see page 41).

Have everything ready before you start. For this project you will need a stepladder that is sturdy and tall enough to allow you to work easily and safely. If you have to stretch you won't be able to work fluently or see what you are doing.

Here a picture rail provides the horizontal alignment. If there isn't a ready-made horizontal, measure down from the ceiling and use a spirit level to establish a base line. You could also use the ceiling or the base of the cornice as the alignment.

Offer the stencil up to the wall and centre the end motif on the corner. Remember that the corner may not be a true vertical, so ensure that the base of the template sits on the base line – otherwise you will find that the border begins to slope.

The methods of applying paint are described on pages 34–37. Here a stippling technique is used to give a flat, even coverage which shows the design off to advantage. Put a pool of paint on a palette. The paint should be of a creamy consistency. You will need a small stencil mottler to get paint into the corner and a larger, round stippler for the more accessible areas. Load the brush with paint as described on page 34 and knock it out on the palette. Practise on lining paper before you start.

1 Establish a base line. Push the stencil plate into the corner, centring the motif on the corner, if possible. The paper stencil plate with its protective coating of cellulose paint is surprisingly tough and flexible. Ensure that the base of the plate rests neatly on the base line. Fix it with masking tape.

2 Working from a palette, load a small stencil mottler with paint. Knock out the brush on the palette – it must not be overloaded. Begin to apply paint in the corner using a tapping motion.

Start with a thin application of colour, gradually building up to the required density.

Corners

The most 'important' corner of a room is the one you see when you enter. First impressions are important so avoid awkward junctions of corner and border pattern at that point.

This stencil has been painted in a single colour, but it could be painted in several colours. You don't need a separate stencil for each one as different colours can be applied through different apertures in the same stencil plate. For an example of this see the floorcloth on page 60.

If you are working in several colours you will need a separate brush for each one.

3 Change to a round stippling brush for the more accessible areas. Load the brush with paint and knock it out as before. Apply the paint with a regular, tapping motion. You will soon find a comfortable working rhythm. Use a brush of the correct size or progress will be slow.

4 Remove the stencil plate to reveal the neat, crisply defined pattern. The stencilled pattern provides its own register for repeats. The stencil plate is dropped over the final painted motif. Check that the plate is resting on the base line and fix it to the wall with masking tape. Continue around the wall.

PLANNING AND SETTING OUT

You Will Need

•

Masking tape
Chalk, metal tape
measure, plumbline
Chalk line, chalk
powder refill
Spirit level, metal
straight-edge
These are all shown in
the picture below.

•

When stencilling on floors or walls you may need vertical or horizontal lines against which the stencil can be aligned. The easiest method is to use existing architectural features such as a dado, picture rail or floorboards, but remember that floors sometimes slope and walls are rarely square. To use an existing alignment cut the stencil plate with an extra border so that the plate butts up to the edge of the alignment. If the stencil is already cut you can paste a strip of paper of the required width to the edge of the plate. For example, the pineapple stencil on page 52 has been cut to the exact width of the stripe and the border stencil on page 38 allows for a 5cm (2 inch) gap between the painted border and the picture rail. If there are no convenient alignments you may have to set out your own.

Establishing a true vertical. You do this with a plumb line – a string with a balanced weight or bob on the end. Run the string over a piece of chalk then pin or tape it to the top of the drop. Allow the bob to swing free – it comes to rest on the vertical. A chalk line can be used in the same way, the chalk box acting as a bob. The string is then 'snapped' to mark the vertical. Blow excess chalk powder away before you apply paint.

Establishing a horizontal line. To find the line for a border at dado-rail height take a measurement from the floor and use a spirit level to establish the horizontal. To establish a horizontal for a frieze, measure from the ceiling and use the spirit level to mark out the horizontal line.

Setting out an all-over pattern. First impressions are important so the best place to start an all-over pattern is usually in the middle of the wall facing the door. However, the focus of the room may be a fireplace which isn't opposite the doorway, and in this case the

Equipment for setting out
The chalk line is a box containing string on a reel and powdered chalk – usually white, blue or red. It is used to mark out long straight lines which are easily erased. Use white chalk on pale grounds to avoid contaminating the paint.

A plumb line is a piece of string with a balanced weight or bob which is used to find true verticals. You can make your own with string and a weight. The spirit level allows you to find a true horizontal by adjusting the level so that the bubble of air settles in the centre of the bulb.

Using a chalk line
Using a chalk line is usually a two-person job. One holds the box and the other holds the end of the string so that it is stretched taut across the surface to be marked. One person 'snaps' the string by pulling it away from the surface and letting go. When the string hits the surface a powdery line is deposited. If you have to work on your own, tape or pin the string to the surface firmly. Unwind the string and pull it taut. Hold the box to the surface with one hand and snap the line with the other.

design should be centred on the chimney breast to avoid asymmetry in a prominent location. Find the centre of the wall area by measurement and establish a vertical using a plumb line. Mark it with a chalk line. Work down the wall, registering repeats on the painted area above. Then return to the top and work down again registering on the adjacent painted area as well as the area above.

Managing the corner: all-over designs. The Pugin all-over design on page 71 illustrates this process clearly. You get as near to the corner as you can and then take the plate around the corner. The oiled and cellulose-painted stencil plate is remarkably resilient and can be pushed right into the corner. Use a small mottler to get the paint into the corner.

Filling gaps in an all-over design. Gaps left at the top and bottom of a wall stencilled with an all-over design may be difficult to fill with the full-size stencil plate. The *All-Over Wall Pattern* illustrates the use of a single-motif stencil to fill these gaps (see pages 72–73). The small stencil is easy to manipulate and for really difficult areas can be trimmed so that it butts right up to the edge.

Managing the corner: borders. With very simple or very narrow designs you can run the stencil plate around the corner. With bigger patterns like the frieze on the previous page you need a more considered solution. By starting the stencil in the corner you see as you enter the room, it was possible to ensure that it worked neatly at that point. Another solution is to design a 'stop' which could be a simple vertical line. This ensures that the border finishes neatly at the corners, saves bending your stencil and gives the impression that the border has been designed for that room.

Setting out a floor. Centre the pattern on the most obvious part of the floor — the part you see on entering or the seating area. Find the centre of this area by establishing diagonals from the corners. If the room is not a simple rectangle break its shape down into its component rectangles. Use a chalk line to mark the diagonals. Establish and mark a vertical alignment and work from the centre of the room (see page 80).

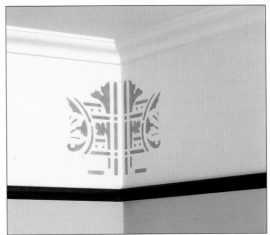

Using a 'stop'

A 'stop' is a device which stops a border neatly, just short of a corner. Here a stop has been made for the border on page 39. A rule has been added to the template which is then used as a stencil — generally the template should not be used as a stencil. In the picture above, the template is taped to the wall and the end motif plus the stop is stencilled using a stippling technique. The template is removed and cleaned and then applied to the other wall — this time the template is flopped to create a mirror image. You can see the result above left. The corner from page 39 is reproduced on the left so that you can compare the two solutions.

To continue the border from a stopped corner register the stencil plate on the end motif and continue working. The design can be picked up on the other wall in the same way.

PROTECTING AND REPAIRING STENCILS

Cutting stencils takes time and effort so it is worth looking after them. A well-made stencil will last a lifetime.

Protecting the stencil. Oiled paper is relatively fragile so the cut stencil must be given a protective coating. Traditionally shellac was used but cellulose paints like Hammerite or car-spray paints are much tougher.

Apply the varnish or paint to both sides of the plate. Stencils which are intended for heavy use should be given two coats of cellulose paint. For example, the stencils for the Moroccan tile projects on pages 94 and 98 were given two coats of Hammerite because the texture-compound/paint mix is heavy and tough on the plates.

Repairing stencils. The ties are the most fragile part of a stencil plate and are vulnerable to breakage. They can be repaired very easily using PVC (electrical) tape. Trim the tape carefully to make a neat mend which doesn't interrupt the line of the pattern. Seal the mended area with cellulose paint.

Storing templates and stencils. If a stencil plate is lost or damaged it can be re-created from the template so it is worth filing your templates away. Templates are easier to store than stencils because they are light and take up very little space. Keep them flat so that they don't get creased or torn.

Stencils must be stored and handled carefully to avoid breaking the delicate ties. One method is to lay them flat in drawers. Dust the plates with talcum powder to stop them from sticking to each other. If you place them between sheets of paper this will prevent the ties from becoming tangled and broken.

The best storage system is the one that minimizes the amount of handling. If you can, hang the plates from nails, avoiding locations where they may be damaged. Because the plates are on view they are easily located.

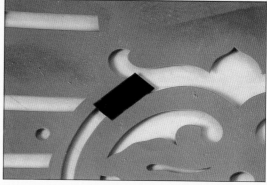

Repairing stencils
1 The ties on some stencils are very delicate and may be broken. This can happen in storage, or as they are handled or used. The broken tie shown here is part of the border stencil plate (inset on the opposite page).

2 You will need a piece of PVC (electrical) tape. Cut it to approximately the correct size and apply it to the break. Rub gently to get a good bond.

Protecting stencils
Shellac varnish can be
applied to stencils which
are intended for light use
only. Otherwise use a
cellulose paint such as
Hammerite or car spray.
Apply the paint to one
side using a decorator's
brush. Leave the stencil to
dry — one hour at most —
and paint the other side.
If necessary apply another
coat of paint to each side.
Clean the brush in
cellulose thinners.

4 Now apply a piece of
tape to this side of the
stencil plate. Turn the
plate over and trim the
tape as in Step 3.

3 Turn the plate over and
using a sharp scalpel trim
the PVC tape neatly so
that the stencil plate
retains its crisp contours.

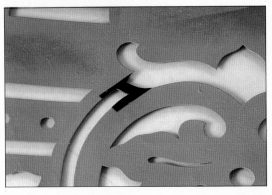

5 Apply a protective film
of cellulose paint to the
area of the break. Do this
on both sides of the
stencil plate and hang the
plate up to dry.

TIPS OF THE TRADE

Brushes. You can make a stippling brush from a French decorator's brush. Bind the bristles tightly with PVC tape and trim the ends of the bristles with a scalpel or sharp scissors. For effective stippling you need a firm brush. The bristles of a round stencilling brush can be stiffened by binding them tightly with PVC tape, just below the ferrule.

Finishes. Varnishes and polishes have two functions. They provide a protective film and also modify the appearance of a surface. Several layers of polyurethane varnish would create a durable surface suitable for a painted floor, while wax polish imparts a mellow glow to stained wood.

Shellac is a natural resin which is used to produce various kinds of varnish including button polish. Brushes should be cleaned in methylated spirits.

Polyurethane is a tough oil-based varnish available in tinted or clear forms. Clear polyurethane has a yellowish tinge and darkens with age. Brushes should be cleaned in turpentine or white spirit.

Acrylic varnish is water-based and colourless and does not yellow with age. Brushes are cleaned in water.

Beeswax is polish which can be applied directly to wood or over varnish. For a smooth finish rub a varnished surface with fine wire wool before applying the wax with a soft cloth.

Textures. A range of textured mediums for use with artist's acrylic paints can be used with household emulsion paints. In the project on page 76 we used a medium called Resin Sand Texture Gel produced by Liquitex.

Texture compounds for covering walls and ceilings are available in the form of powders. A mixture of emulsion paint and texture compound applied through a stencil plate can be used to create relief effects such as the tiles on page 92 and the stone effect on page 104.

Making a stippling brush
A good quality stippling brush can be made by cutting down a round French decorator's brush. Tape the bristles firmly with PVC tape and trim the bristles to one length with a sharp knife or scalpel.

Finishes
In this picture we show three coloured French enamels — green and blue in the shallow dishes and red in the ridged bottle. The small dish at the top contains beeswax and beside it there is a rag for applying the wax. Methylated spirit (in the plastic bottle) is the solvent for shellac-based varnishes like button polish (in the square pot at the bottom). Turpentine (in the white pot, left) or white spirit are the solvents for polyurethane varnish (in the large pot at the bottom).

Mixing texture compound

Use approximately 4 parts texture compound to 1 part emulsion paint and water. Put the texture compound powder in a pot, add the paint and mix thoroughly. Add water to achieve a consistency which is stiff enough to form peaks. The texture compound will lighten the colour of the paint but a final coat of varnish will restore its intensity.

Sanding

Different sandpapers are used for different purposes. It is worth buying a good quality paper as it will last longer and give a better result. The most durable sandpapers are aluminium oxide resin-bonded sandpapers (the yellow and green papers, left). They are available in a range from 40 (coarse) to 120 (fine). Silicon carbide paper, known as wet and dry sandpaper, is used to achieve a fine finish. It ranges from 120 to 1000. The water stops the paper becoming clogged up with particles. A power sander is useful but not necessary.

Storing stencils

The shallow shelves of a plan chest provide ideal storage but stencils can also be hung from beams, or battens on the wall. Punch two holes in each stencil – use a hole punch to make neat holes without tearing the stencil. By spacing the holes to match the nails you can ensure that the stencil hangs flat.

TRADITIONAL SCANDINAVIAN FOLK ART

The most appealing aspect of the Scandinavian look is the way strong, folk designs are combined with a palette of colours which are both subtle and intense. These include all the earth shades – reds, browns and golden yellows – as well as a range of blue-greens and greeny-blues. These colours are often described as muted, 'knocked back' or dulled, but this does not mean that they are insipid, as the cheerful kitchen on the opposite page shows. Its walls are brightened with a bold stripe and stylized pineapple motif, the cabinets enlivened with a hand-drawn leaf stencil.

Bold fruit and leaf stencil designs derived from folk art are combined with a cool northern blue in this tranquil Scandinavian-style kitchen.

CUPBOARD WITH A
SIMPLE LEAF MOTIF

This is a simple design based on a single motif. The design was drawn freehand – the template can be found on page 133. The first thing to decide is how big the motif should be. It is tempting to be tentative when you are applying a single design, 'just in case it doesn't work'. But nothing is as unsatisfactory as a half-hearted decoration, so if in doubt make the motif a little larger than feels right. Some people naturally have a good eye for design; others lack confidence and spend so much time planning that they end up doing nothing at all. Be bold – your first idea is often the best.

To explore the effects achieved by different-sized motifs, and different locations, do a sketch of the motif on cartridge paper. Trace off several copies and enlarge or reduce them. Colour them in roughly, then tape the pieces of paper in place using masking tape. You should position the leaves by eye, but if in doubt you will find that a loca-

You Will Need

●

Stencil plate from template
p.133
Oil or emulsion paint: a muted
leaf green
Medium stippling brush
Palette
Masking tape
Chalk

●

tion on the third division of any space is generally the most satisfying. For 'random' effects like this, avoid pure symmetry. It doesn't suit the naturalistic design. Live with the sketches for a few days. Seeing them as you pass is a good test of whether they are right. You could also explore different colours.

Use a stippling technique to apply the paint (see page 34). It is important that the brush is not overloaded so don't work straight from the paint pot. Put the paint on a palette and load the brush from that. Then 'knock it out' to remove excess paint. It is better to have too little paint on your brush than too much. You have more control and the paint layer can be built up gradually by going over it several times. This may be more time-consuming, but is safer than overloading the brush so that the paint seeps under the edge of the stencil. Use your left hand to hold the stencil plate close to the wall.

1 Your surface should be clean and dry. Make a chalk mark at the point at which you want to locate the stencil. Fix the stencil plate to the surface with masking tape.

2 Load the brush with paint from the palette, then knock the paint out so that the brush is not overloaded. Apply the paint with a light tapping motion, holding the stencil plate close to the surface so that paint does not seep under it.

Tip
You can make your own leaf stencil very easily. Find an interesting leaf – an oak leaf, or a large, lobed sycamore leaf, for example, and lay it on a sheet of good quality cartridge paper. Trace the shape with a pencil, then cut and prepare the stencil (see page 32).

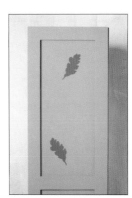

3 Lift off the stencil plate and apply it in the next location, working as described above. The illustrations here and opposite show just how effective a single, simple motif can be.

BREAD POT WITH A
THREE-COLOUR LEAF MOTIF

This is a variation on a single, repeated stencil motif, in which the leaf is given a suggestion of form by using three closely related colours. These are applied through the same stencil plate. In a kitchen setting it could be used as here on a pot; it could also be used to enliven a tray or other storage container. Shades of green have been chosen to tie the leaf in with the previous motif and because it is a natural leaf colour. However, that isn't the only solution. Here, for example, the blue/aqua colour of the cabinets could have been used equally successfully on the pot. These typically Scandinavian cool blues and blue-greens work particularly well against the warm, pinkish tones of terracotta. You could create the three tones by tinting a basic green emulsion with acrylic paint.

Again, the technique is very simple but, as most of the work has to be done by eye, it is a good idea to practise before you start. However, don't worry about mistakes –

they simply add to the charm of the effect, and give it that special hand-crafted look. If you do make what you think of as a mistake, keep it to yourself. People will only notice if you draw attention to it.

For this project three related colours are applied, shifting the stencil very slightly between applications. If you are putting the stencil around a pot, measure the pot's circumference and divide it by an even number – say four or six – and mark off these points in chalk. With an even number, the design can be alternated so that one leaf points up, the next one down. With an odd number, all the motifs should point in the same direction.

This technique of putting two or three related tones of a colour through the same stencil can be used to give any simple stencil design a new twist. It works best with designs which are based on natural forms as it creates a suggestion of three dimensions.

You Will Need

•

Stencil plate from template
p.133
3 related shades of paint: light,
medium, dark. Emulsion or
acrylic paints are best as they
are quick-drying
3 mottlers, one for each colour
Palette
Masking tape
Terracotta pot or container

•

1 Tape the stencil plate to the container. Put some of each colour on the palette and load a stencil mottler with the mid-tone colour, knocking it out on the palette to prevent overloading. Apply the paint with a stippling motion for even coverage.

2 Take the stencil plate off. When the paint is touch dry replace the plate so that it overlaps the design on one side, exposing about 3mm (1/8 inch) of unpainted surface on the other. Apply the lightest colour, working from the edge towards the centre, gradating the colour.

3 Remove the plate and wait until the second colour is touch dry. Replace the plate, this time shifting it in the other direction so that a sliver of the bare surface shows through as before. Apply the darkest colour, working from the unpainted edge towards the centre. Try to grade the colour by applying less paint as you move towards the centre. Remove the plate. The three colours should merge into one another, creating the effect of light shining on a curved surface. Repeat the motif around the container

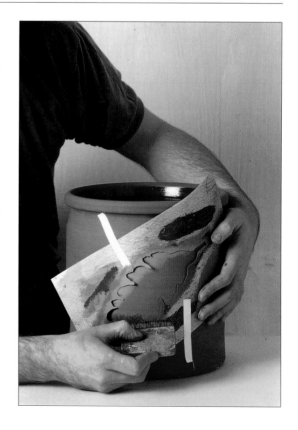

1 Centre the stencil
plate on the stripe
and tape in place. Stipple
the green paint on both
motifs, pushing the plate
against the surface and
making sure paint reaches
into all the intricate
angles. Then stipple the
yellow ochre on the
bodies of the pineapples.

2 The lower pineapple
provides the register
for the second move.
Place the plate so that the
upper motif on the plate
sits over the lower painted
pineapple. Fix the plate to
the wall with masking tape
and proceed as before.

A Pineapple
Striped Wall

Here, a bold pineapple motif is stencilled on a kitchen wall for a bright and cheerful look – the inspiration was a pineapple print in a magazine. The wall was painted in off-white and stripes 40cm (15 3/4 inches) wide were measured on to it. Alternate stripes were masked with masking tape, using a plumb line to establish the vertical, and then painted in a wash of cream and pale blue.

There are many ways in which the pineapple motif could be used. It could, for example, be applied to a single base colour without the stripes. Alternatively, it could be applied to, say, the cream stripes but not the blue.

The finished stencil is given a hand-painted look by applying criss-cross lines to describe the faceted surface of the pineapple. The easiest and most effective way to do this is to use a piece of torn card. Dip it into the paint on a palette and then run it lightly across the pineapples'

You Will Need

•

Stencil plate from template
p.133
Emulsion or acrylic paint: dark
green, dark brown, yellow ochre
2 medium-size round French
stipplers
Palette
Masking tape
Lightweight card with a torn
edge

•

surface. Swiftness and a sure touch will give the best results, so practise on lining paper until you get just the right effect.

The choice of colours is important. Avoid the temptation to use a bright yellow – not only are pineapples a muted mustard yellow, but slightly subdued colours are easier on the eye. Similarly, avoid too bright a green – it will simply be overpowering. Use instead a slightly dull forest or sage green. Too bright a green can be darkened with a touch of a reddish brown or acrylic burnt sienna. Some greens can be knocked back with black, but care is needed as black can be a very deadening colour. Yellow can be muted with a touch of its complementary colour, violet. Practise these mixes on lining paper painted with the base colours that are to be used on the walls.

To simplify the stencilling process cut the stencil plate to the exact width of the stripe. The edge of the plate can then be aligned on the edge of the stripe.

3 Dip the torn edge of the card in the brown paint and make brisk, parallel diagonals over the pineapple body, then work in the other direction to create a grid of diamond shapes.

4 The motif can be used in any number of ways. You could, for example, make the pineapples quite small, alternate a row of small pineapples with larger ones, or use a single pineapple motif in the middle of a cupboard door or a chair seat.

SIMPLE 'MODERNE' STYLE

I n the early part of this century architects and designers throughout the world sought to devise a style which broke with the past and reflected the spirit of the machine age. This was expressed in simpler forms, a use of new materials and a reaction against excessive ornament. The inspiration for the stencil designs here was the 'jazzy' geometry of a piece of coloured glass discovered in a street market. It has been used to create a floorcloth design. This is teamed with a contemporary cabinet which is a direct descendant of the furniture which seemed so revolutionary in the 1920s and 1930s.

A functional cabinet in light wood has been cleverly transformed into an 'inlaid' masterpiece using a stencil and artist's oil paint.

CABINET WITH A
WOOD INLAY EFFECT

This project demonstrates how you can enhance the plainest object and give your home that considered, designer look for a minimal outlay. It typifies the two pleasures of stencilling: the enjoyment of the creative process itself and the lasting appeal of an object which you have decorated and made your own.

Oil paint is applied to wood through a stencil plate. The paint is then rubbed with a cloth whilst still wet so that it creates a transparent film, staining the wood rather than covering it. The paint builds up around the margins of the stencil plate openings, creating crisply defined edges which enhance the 'inlaid' effect.

The technique has many applications. Small items decorated in this way make lovely gifts. For instance, a plain wooden tray or box can be transformed into something unique and precious-looking by applying a stylized foliate motif or a classical swag and urn rondel.

You Will Need

●

Stencil plate 1: border, from template p.134
Stencil plate 2: all-over trellis, from template p.134
Alkyd paints: black, Van Dyke brown
2 small stippling brushes, one for each colour
Palette
Masking tape, guard
Soft cotton cloth
White spirit
Plain wooden cabinet or chest

●

When looking for stencils to use in this way, concentrate on stylized and geometric designs which capture the character of inlaid wood. The source for this stencil was a book on Viennese design.

The paints used here are fast-drying artist's oils, called alkyds. The same effect could be achieved with traditional artist's oil paint, but you would have to allow several weeks for the paint to dry sufficiently to take the final application of varnish or polish. Alkyds are entirely compatible with oil paint and, like oil, they are thinned with turpentine or white spirit.

The project is carried out in two stages using two stencils. The border is applied first so that it can be masked while the all-over trellis pattern is applied to the top. It would be much more difficult to do it the other way round: you would still have to mask the border, but you would have to be careful to make sure that it butted up neatly to the trellis.

1 Align the midpoint of stencil plate 1 with the midpoint of one long side of the cabinet. Fix the plate to the cabinet with masking tape. Stipple on the black paint, allowing it to build up around the edges of the plate openings.

2 With the soft cotton cloth, rub the paint in the centre of each plate opening. This pushes the paint into the grain of the wood and also removes excess paint.

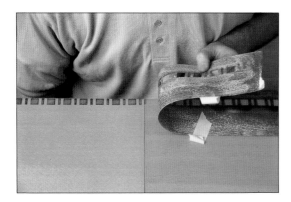

3 Move the plate to do the next section, registering it on a section of the already stencilled border. Tape the plate in position and continue as above. Repeat until one side is completed. Work the opposite side in the same way, followed by the shorter sides.

4 Allow the paint to dry thoroughly – overnight should be enough – then mask it with masking tape

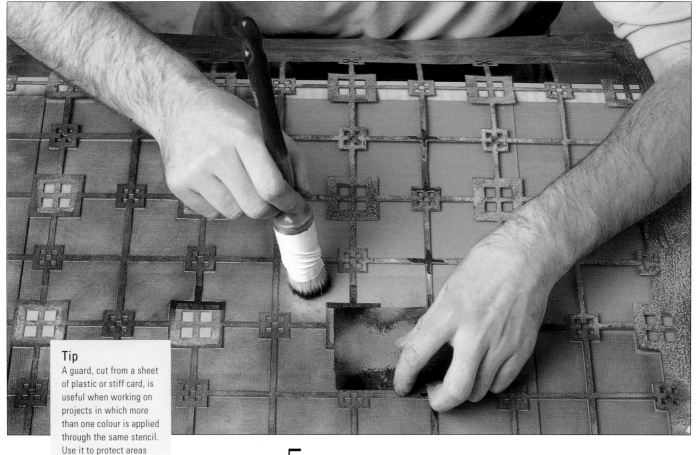

Tip
A guard, cut from a sheet of plastic or stiff card, is useful when working on projects in which more than one colour is applied through the same stencil. Use it to protect areas that have already been painted and those to be painted another colour.

5 Position stencil plate 2 in the centre of the top of the cabinet. Stipple a thin, even layer of the brown paint through the large openings in the plate, using a 'guard' to protect the non-Van Dyke-brown areas. Here filling knives are used as guards. They are ideal for this purpose.

6 Rub back the paint with the cloth, as in Stage 2. Work all the brown areas before applying the black paint to the four small squares in the middle of the motif.

7 Stipple black paint on to the squares in the middle of the motif, guarding the previously worked areas. You might find it easier to use a smaller brush for these details.

8 Move the stencil plate, registering it on a previously stencilled area, and continue working as above until the surface is complete. Allow the paint to dry before finishing with varnish or polish. A functional cabinet has been transformed into something that could pass for the work of a skilled craftsman.

AN *ART DECO*
FLOORCLOTH

Floorcloths are practical, beautiful to look at and fun to make. They first became popular in the early eighteenth century, when they were painted to imitate marble or marquetry. Later they were often stencilled.

The design for this floorcloth was taken from a piece of glass found in a London street market. Its bold, geometric patterns and lovely colours are typical of 1930s design. Eau-de-Nil, silver-grey and earth reds are given solidity by the patches of black.

The stencil was created by using a sheet of gridded acetate to scale up the design directly on to the stencil plate, avoiding the template stage (see page 28). If you find a design you like, a piece of stained glass or a textile, for example, it can be translated into a stencil plate as described below (see also page 28). If you want to re-create this stencil plate using the template on page 135, start at Stage 4.

Notice that all four colours are applied through the same

You Will Need

●

Stencil plate from template
p.135
Emulsion paint: black, terracotta,
eau-de-Nil, silver-grey
Brushes: 2 mottlers and 2 small
stippling brushes
Palette
Guards
Masking tape
Cotton canvas, tacks or staples
Acrylic varnish
Glue or double-sided tape

●

stencil plate. It is best if you have a separate brush for each colour. You will need guards – filling knives, bits of plastic or card – to protect one area as you work on another. It is particularly important to use an acrylic varnish on a pale design such as the one in this project as oil varnish tends to yellow with age.

The stencil plate consists of two triangular corner motifs. Use them as they are shown here; alternatively, use just one motif on the four corners of a rectangle, or even in just one corner. This motif would also work well on a table top, or it could be applied directly to a wood or hardboard floor. You could even make a single square design by butting two triangles up against each other.

If you want to change the colourways to suit your own room, experiment by trying them out first on lining paper. If you are using the stencil for a large floorcloth, simply tape several sheets of lining paper together.

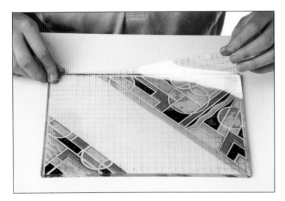

1 'Grid up' your stencil plate from the original design. Transfer the design to a piece of acetate when the source is too valuable to be drawn on. Here, the acetate has been ruled up into 1cm (3/8 inch) squares.

2 Divide the cartridge paper into the same number of squares as the acetate and transfer the image square by square. Curves can be drawn by hand, or a found object can be used as a guide. Here, a roll of masking tape was just right for one of the circles.

3 Cut the stencil plate as described on page 32. Then seal it with shellac or metallic paint. Shellac was used here as the plate is not intended for heavy use.

4 Fix the sheet of canvas to the floor using tacks or staples, lay on the base colour and allow to dry. Tape the first corner stencil plate in place and stipple on the black paint. Then apply the terracotta, using a guard to protect adjacent sections.

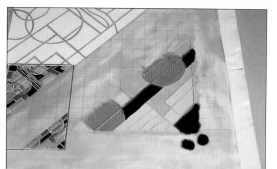

5 Apply the other colours in turn, again using a guard to protect adjacent sections.

6 Once the first corner is complete, rule in the rectangle to position the motif correctly in the opposite corner.

7 Work the second corner in the same way as the first one. Here, two guards are used to mask intricate areas before the first colour, black, is applied.

8 Once both motifs are complete, protect the edges with masking tape and paint a border if desired. To finish, apply 3–4 layers of acrylic varnish to build up a hard-wearing surface. Turn in a narrow seam and glue or fix with double-sided tape.

HIGH VICTORIAN GOTHIC DESIGN

T ime and again artists, architects and designers have returned to the Middle Ages for inspiration. Eighteenth-century 'Gothick' was a light-hearted and frivolous pastiche of medievalism which gave rise to a delight in the 'picturesque', sham ruins and follies. A hundred years later the Victorians returned to the Middle Ages in a less fanciful way. The most prolific, brilliant and eccentric of the Victorian 'medievalizers' was Augustus Welby Northmore Pugin (1812-52). He promoted an integrated approach to design that revolutionized taste, and provided much of the foundation for the Arts and Crafts Movement.

In this comfortable Victorian Gothic study a Pugin wallpaper has been re-created using an all-over stencil — it is a look which never goes out of fashion.

LAMPSHADE WITH A
BORDER MOTIF

This project is both simple and effective and illustrates the way in which stencilling can be used to carry a particular theme throughout a room. The motif has been taken from the intricate, all-over pattern illustrated on page 71; two elements from that design have been combined to create a repeating border. As with all the templates provided, the one for this motif can be used to create a stencil plate of the same size, or it can be gridded up or enlarged on a photocopier.

Once the stencil plate is made (see page 32), there are many ways in which it could be used. With fabric paint, a pretty border could be made for muslin or plain fabric curtains; enlarged, it could be used to create a border between upper wall and dado; or applied as a single motif, it could decorate a chair seat or cushion cover. Even the single fleur-de-lis motif from the middle of the design could be taken on its own to create a related but different pattern.

You Will Need
●

Stencil plate from template
p.136
Emulsion or acrylic paint: green
Small stippling brush
Palette
Masking tape

●

The first problem is how to make the border fit your shade. You could work it out mathematically but there is no need. Just start at the seam and use the 'wings' on the stencil to ensure that the motifs are evenly spaced. When the border comes back to the seam simply finish with a part-motif – the seam will be turned away from the viewer in use. Use a constant such as the base of the shade or the seam to align the base of the stencil.

Colour is an important aspect of putting any design together. Here, rich Victorian greens are combined with dark Gothic furniture. The lampshade was designed to team with a green ceramic lampbase. But if you have a slender candlestick-type lampbase why not introduce a touch of gold, with gold detailing on the base picked up in a gold border on the shade? It would look especially dramatic on a black lampshade – see the tray on page 68 for an example of these colours in combination.

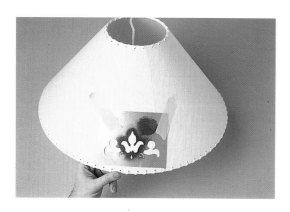

1 Position the stencil plate on the shade. Find something to align it on – it may be the base, or a stitched hem; with this shade it was the seam and punched holes around the base. Fix the stencil plate in position with masking tape.

2 Holding the shade firmly with one hand, stipple the paint through the plate, building the paint up to the density you want. Allow the paint to dry – a matter of seconds – and lift the stencil plate from the shade.

3 Position the stencil plate for the next motif by butting up one of its 'wings' against the first motif and aligning it on the base, hem or seam as appropriate. This is a simple, no-measuring way of ensuring even spacing of the motifs.

Tip

For greater space between motifs, allow a bigger 'wing' when drawing the stencil. Or make a spacer bar – a piece of card cut to the width of the space required. If you want 4 cm (1 1/2 inches) between motifs cut a spacer bar to that width. Each time you move the stencil plate, simply lay the spacer bar alongside the previous motif and align the stencil plate against it. It is a quick and effective way of working.

4 Fix the stencil in place with masking tape and apply paint as before. Work round the shade until you return to the first motif, finishing at the seam with a part-motif. This will not be distracting as we are used to patterned textiles and printed papers which meet in this way on a seam.

With its restrained border picking up the Gothic theme of the room, a modern lampshade is able to sit comfortably within a Victorian Gothic setting.

2 Stipple gold paint from the palette through the register mark apertures and the motif, making the film of paint on the latter as even as possible. Allow the paint to dry – about 20 minutes. Leave stencil plate 1 in position.

1 Place stencil plate 1 in the visual centre of the tray and fix it in position with masking tape. Lifting the edges of the plate, put Post-it notes on the tray under the register mark apertures.

Tip
Masking tape or Post-it notes are useful for making register marks without applying paint to the surface. Locate the first stencil and place the masking tape or Post-it note under the register. Apply paint through the register aperture.

3 Stipple black gouache through the motif of plate 1 until all the gold is completely covered. Do not paint over the register marks. Leave to dry – about 10 minutes. Remove plate 1.

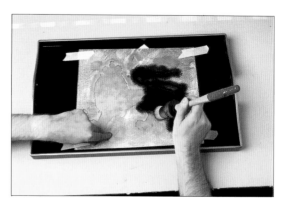

HERALDIC
TRAY

This tray was decorated using a 'wipe-out' technique devised by W. W. Davidson in the 1920s. It allows you to create images with soft edges and a painterly feel which is very different from the crisp and mechanical appearance of an ordinary stencil. Two stencil plates are required: the first, and slightly larger of the two, a simple 'silhouette' of the motif; the second, and smaller one, a plate of the motif details. The main colour, in this case gold, is applied through the first plate. Then, with the plate still in position, the gold is completely covered by the second colour: black gouache. The first plate is then replaced with the second. The gouache, now showing through the cut details on the second plate, is moistened with a damp brush and then rubbed back gently with a soft cloth to reveal the gold underneath.

Register marks, paint applied through small triangles cut in both stencil plates in exactly the same place, make

You Will Need

●

Stencil plate 1: silhouette of lion, from template p.136
Stencil plate 2: details of lion, from template p.136
Gold powder and shellac, or metallic gold paint.
Black gouache
2 medium-size round stippling brushes and a palette
Masking tape, Post-it notes
Soft cotton cloth
Shellac polish or varnish
Lacquer tray

●

it possible to position the second, smaller plate correctly. However, since these marks are only temporary and must not damage the surface, they are applied to masking tape or a Post-it note (as in this project) set under each aperture when the first plate is positioned. Once the work is complete, these can be peeled off.

Representational designs such as figures, fruit, flowers or foliage lend themselves to this treatment because the variations of tone suggest form. Fruits, vegetables and flowers would work well in a kitchen setting, while animals, characters from nursery rhymes and story books would make a lovely frieze for a child's room. Experiment with different colourways: the sumptuous gold and black used here was suggested by the colours of the lacquer tray and the Gothic setting. However, jewel-bright primary colours, for instance, would capture the vigour of 1930s illustrations or the brilliance of stained glass.

4 Position plate 2, aligning the marks on the Post-it notes with the register marks on the plate. With a damp brush work up the gouache, then gently rub some of it off with the cloth. Remove plate 2, but leave the Post-it notes in place.

5 Replace plate 1 using the register marks and stipple shellac polish through the motif. Oil or spray varnish could also be used. With a spray, however, the rest of the tray should be masked to protect the lacquer finish. Remove the stencil plate and Post-it notes.

ALL-OVER WALL
PATTERN

This stencil is based on a piece of wallpaper by the great Victorian designer Augustus Pugin who began designing wallpapers in the 1840s. It is an intricate pattern based on medallions and foliate motifs, and combines a tracery of fine lines with patches of solid colour. Stencilling offers a wonderful way of creating exactly the wallcovering you want and for very little cost. Not only can you have precisely the right design for the effect you are aiming to create, you can also choose the colours. And when you redecorate you can use the design in different colourways.

Here a solid but muted holly green on a sage green ground enhances the Victorian feel of the pattern. This combination of colours gives enough contrast for the pattern to read without it dancing before the eyes. The colours you choose will depend on the effect you are seeking to achieve, the location in which the pattern will be seen, the type and amount of light and the scale at

You Will Need

●

Stencil plate from template p.137, plus a single motif (see Stage 3)
Emulsion paint in 2 colours: one for the base coat, the second for the stencil
Large stippling brush for the main area, small stippling brush for the single motif
Palette
Masking tape, chalk line

●

which you cut the pattern. For a more subtle effect, choose colours which are closer in tone; alternatively, deliberately emphasize the contrast by using, for example, red over green. It is worth experimenting: the number of effects that can be achieved with a single stencil design is startling.

When preparing to cut the stencil plate, decide how many repeats you want to make. Obviously, the bigger the plate, the faster you can work; but the longer the plate will take to cut. The plate used here had 13 repeats. However, if you find cutting plates tedious, simply go for five. Do not worry about slips of the knife. These 'mistakes' will be repeated and become part of the pattern.

When applying the plate, start at the top in the middle of the wall facing the door. Work downwards, lapping the plate over the motif above; then move to the side and work down, lapping the plate over the motif to the side and also the one above. Then work into the corner.

1 Mask picture rail, skirting board, door and window frames. In the centre of the wall facing the door mark the vertical using a chalk line (see page 40). Align the stencil against this and the base of the picture rail and fix it with tape. Stipple on colour with the large stippling brush.

2 Work down, overlapping the medallions at the top of the plate with those at the bottom of the painted area. Then move to the side, again overlapping medallions on the plate with those already painted.

3 Work as far into the corner as possible. Use the plate of the single motif to fill the gap, as shown. To fill the gap where the ceiling or picture rail meets the corner, the plate will have to be cut, so leave these sections until last.

4 Use the small plate to fill the spaces between the ceiling or picture rail and the main pattern. Fix the plate with masking tape and, holding it against the wall, apply the paint with a small stippling brush.

5 Fill the spaces along the bottom of the wall in the same way. This filling exercise can be done either as you go along, or at the end.

6 To make sure the pattern butts right up against the picture rail or ceiling, cut the small plate down to fit. Do all four corners if necessary. Apply the paint with a small stippling brush.

7 Fill all the small gaps in this way, cutting the plate down as necessary.

Tip

It is difficult to predict just how the stencil will meet with the skirting board. You will find it easier to work if you overlap more motifs so that you get as near as possible to it. The same applies when working up to or into a corner.

8 Remove the masking tape. With all the gaps filled and the corners rounded, the pattern covers the walls without interruption.

MEDIEVAL HERALDIC STYLE

The Middle Ages has a strong hold on our collective imagination. Artists, writers and designers have found inspiration in the rich imagery and romance of the medieval world. This was the age of chivalry, of courtly love and wandering troubadours. A love of rich ornament was combined with spartan living conditions. Walls were plastered and painted or hung with elaborate tapestries. Floors were decorated with tiles in various patterns. Here, the essence of the period has been captured in a manner which sits comfortably with the most modern designs.

The old and the new are pleasingly combined in this living room in which rich medieval ornament provides a foil for contemporary design.

1 Begin by plotting the positions of the motifs. Here the bigger motifs were located at the ends and centre of the fireplace with the smaller motifs between them. The arrangement shown here suited the size of the fireplace and the scale of the stencils. However, a different arrangement may suit your fireplace better. You could, for example, omit the large motif in the middle and simply fill the space between the two end motifs with the small fleur-de-lis designs evenly spaced.

Use a tape measure to find the centre of the fireplace and mark the point with pencil.

2 Place the paint and some of the resin sand on the piece of scrap board or cardboard and mix thoroughly with the trowel. The mixture should be paste-like but easy to spread. If it is too stiff add a little water. Practise applying the paste through the stencil plate on to the sheet of scrap paper. Lift the plate off carefully to create a neat edge. Once you feel comfortable working with the mixture, fix the plate to the fireplace with masking tape and apply the mixture with the plasterer's small tool as shown.

FIREPLACE WITH A
TEXTURED MOTIF

Until the late 1940s the traditional hearth was the centre of the living area and although its practical purpose has been usurped by central heating in most homes, a fireplace is still valued by many as a focus. The matt black surface of this fireplace has been enlivened with a medieval motif in gold, taken from a book on antique textiles.

To give the simple design sparkle, texture was added to the paint. An acrylic texture medium called resin sand, produced by Liquitex, was used. Mixed with the emulsion paint it gives a slightly grainy texture a bit like rough sandpaper. There are a wide range of mediums on the market, designed to modify the appearance of acrylic paint for fine art and craft applications. These can also be used with emulsion paint. Although they are too expensive for large-scale work they can add a new dimension to a simple stencilled motif.

Texture is sometimes undervalued in decorative schemes.

You Will Need

•

Stencil plate 1: floral motif, from
template p.138
Stencil plate 2: fleur-de-lis, from
template p.138
Acrylic paint: yellow ochre
Liquitex texture paste 'resin
sand'
Trowel; plasterer's small tool or
an artist's large painting knife
Piece of scrap board or
cardboard
Masking tape
Tape measure

•

Here the textured surface adds visual interest, makes the motif stand proud of the surface and increases its reflective quality, so that the earth-yellow paint sparkles like gold against the dull, black background.

Simple motifs like these can be used in many ways. If you want to use them on a bigger scale they can be gridded up or enlarged on a photocopier (see page 28). The two motifs can be used together or separately. The smaller fleur-de-lis elements could be made up into a discreet border to define the division between upper wall and dado, or at picture rail level. Because it is neat and delicate it can be used on smaller items – on the backs of straight-backed chairs or around a lampshade, for example (see page 66).

In the same way the larger, stylized floral motif could be combined with the fleur-de-lis in a border or used on its own on a chair back, a bedhead, or applied to the top corners of a rectangular mirror frame.

3 The texture paste dries to give a hard, tough finish. The slightly grainy surface contrasts well with the matt surface of the black background and gives the paint a sparkling, reflective quality.

4 Continue to work in this way, arranging the motifs so that they suit the size and design of your fireplace.

Box Decorated in
Gold, Coral And Blue

The trick to creating medieval appeal is combining lavish treatments and luxurious materials with rather austere surroundings, natural materials and simple shapes. This pine box, transformed with gold paint and a quatrefoil motif in bright clear colours, meets that requirement exactly.

The design here was based on a book on ornament of the Middle Ages. To give an authentically aged effect, the edge has been taken off the colours and the gold dulled by polishing it with slightly tinted button polish (shellac). Alternatively, you could apply a coat of tinted varnish.

For inspiration, study medieval paintings in art galleries or in books. Or look at the exquisitely illuminated books of hours such as *Les Très Riches Heures du Duc de Berry* with its detailed paintings of men and women dressed in gorgeous and richly patterned fabrics. The pattern books of Augustus Pugin, Owen Jones or Christopher Dresser are

You Will Need

•

Stencil plate from template
p.138
Gold paint
Emulsion paint in 2 colours:
coral, blue
Tinted lacquer or varnish
Medium decorating brush for the
gold paint
2 small round stippling brushes
Palette, T-square
Masking tape
Guard, sandpaper
Wooden box or chest

•

also rich in inspiration. Look for the fleur-de-lis, heraldic devices, ogee shapes, and the trefoil and quatrefoil.

One of the recurrent themes is the use of gold – gold thread in textiles, gold leaf on surfaces, in paintings and in illuminated manuscripts. Today many different gold and other metallic materials are available for decorating. There are gold paints in acrylic and gouache ranges, as well as spirit-based ones, or you can use gold powders mixed with a medium such as button polish. Gold paints are generally available in a range of shades, from bronze golds to bright yellow golds. It is worth spending time finding one you like. Remember, though, that a gold that is too yellow or glittery won't look 'authentic'.

Stencilling need not be difficult. Often the ability to choose a style and match it with appropriate colours and textures is more important than technical skill – as the transformation of this wooden box demonstrates.

1 Sandpaper the surfaces of the box until smooth and remove any surface grime. Then paint the box with gold. Here, gold powder mixed with shellac was used.

Tip
Find the centre of the top by drawing two diagonals and dropping a vertical using a T-square. Place the stencil square on the centre. For the next moves, work out from the centre in all directions.

2 Tape the stencil plate to the centre of the box top (see Tip). Stipple on the first colour (coral) using a small round stippling brush. Apply the the second colour (blue) using a guard to protect areas that have already been painted.

3 Here, one move of the stencil plate is complete. Because this stencil plate is large the top can be completed in three moves. A smaller stencil would require more moves.

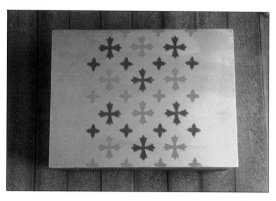

4 Move the plate to one side, using the area already painted to provide a register. Fix the plate in place with masking tape and stipple on the paint as above. Once the top is complete, stencil the sides, bending the plate over and round the edges of the box to create a continuous pattern. When the paint has dried, apply a coat of tinted varnish to 'knock back' the gold.

2 Find the middle of the floor by establishing diagonals from the corner and mark the point with chalk. Align stencil plate 4 on this point and parallel to the floorboards. If the floor isn't boarded, draw a line at right angles to the wall to give an alignment. Apply the paint with the roller.

1 Mask the bottom of the skirting board with tape. Fix stencil plate 1 to the floor with masking tape and apply the black emulsion paint with the roller. Protect the skirting board if necessary with a guard or, as here, a spatula. For the repeat, register the plate on the painted motif. Use plates 2 and 3 for the corners. Once the border is complete and dry, mask its edge with tape to protect it while working on the main area.

3 Work towards one wall. When you reach it, bend the plate so that you can work up to the border edge. Return to the centre of the room and work towards the opposite wall. Then start on a second strip, registering the plate on the painted motif.

80

FLOOR WITH A
GEOMETRIC TILE DESIGN

This complex geometric pattern of interlinking curves and circles is based on one created by the designer and writer Christopher Dresser (1834-1904). He started his career as a botanical illustrator with a particular interest in the geometry of plants and produced several books and papers on aspects of botany. In fact, it was only after he failed to obtain the chair of botany at University College London that he decided to concentrate on the decorative arts and ornament.

He worked with incredible speed producing designs for all kinds of utilitarian and decorative objects from wallpapers and textiles through to ironwork and glass. Most of his work has an underlying austerity and reveals the love of the geometric forms which he had first seen in plant life.

The pattern is complex but satisfying, one form linking with or echoing another in a lively and organic manner. Like all good design this floor pattern is timeless; it works equally well in a period or contemporary setting. Before you start, map out your moves in a sketch – this will make the process a lot easier.

The stencil is teamed with a border, for which there are three parts: the straight border; a 90-degree corner piece for the corners of the room; and a 270-degree corner piece which is used for jutting corners such as a column or around the outer edge of the hearth.

Start by putting in the border, then mask that and work on the main area. In that way you will bring the tile design neatly up to the border. Work the main stencil from the centre of the area. In a rectangular room, you can find the centre by establishing diagonals from the corners and marking the point at which they cross each other. Establish a vertical at this point and use this to align the stencil plate. If you are working on a boarded floor you can use the planks to align against.

> **You Will Need**
>
> ●
>
> Stencil plate 1: straight border, from template p.139
> Stencil plate 2: 90-degree corner, from template p.139
> Stencil plate 3: 270-degree corner, from template p.139
> Stencil plate 4: main motif, from template p.139
> Black emulsion paint
> Gloss sponge roller, palette
> Masking tape, guard, chalk line
> Polyurethane varnish
>
> ●

4 Once you have covered the floor with as many complete workings of the plate as possible, fill in the gaps around, for instance, the hearth. Bend the plate as necessary to reach up to the border edge. (You may find an assistant useful at this stage, to hold the loose edge of the plate and prevent it from flopping over as you work.) When the whole area has been covered and the paint is dry, apply three layers of polyurethane varnish to give a hard-wearing finish.

WALL HANGING WITH A
HERALDIC MOTIF

The monochrome appearance of the interiors of surviving medieval castles bears little relationship to what they originally looked like. What doesn't survive is the rich colour and decoration in the form of wall paintings and tapestries, and textile hangings in coarse linens or the finest silks. Because there was comparatively little furniture, even in grand households, it was the wall decorations and textiles that provided the rich colours and sense of luxury.

Though uncomfortable by our standards, the castles were far less bleak than the cheerless walls which survive today suggest. A wide range of patterns and ornament was used, including designs from nature and heraldic devices like fleur-de-lis, shields and coats of arms. Geometric devices of all sorts were also popular, as were scenes from the Bible and from romances and legends.

For a wall hanging like the one shown here a big, bold

You Will Need

•

Stencil plate from template
p.140
Emulsion paint in 2 colours
Gloss sponge roller
Palette or paint tray
Masking tape
Straight edge
Sharp knife
Canvas

•

design works best. In fact, this is an ideal way of using a pattern which would be overwhelming on wallpaper or even on soft furnishings. A small pattern would simply look like a panel of wallpaper.

Two colours were used: a base colour, and a second colour which was applied through the stencil plate. Experiment with different colour combinations, picking up colours from the rest of the room. Sometimes a splash of colour from a favourite ornament, a carpet or a furnishing fabric can be the key. Often closely related colours make the best partners, but in this case you can afford to be bold; the hanging is there to catch the eye.

Once finished, the panel should hang flat so that the pattern can be seen. Here, it was clipped to a Gothic-style iron curtain pole. Alternatively, make eyelets along the top of the canvas and use rope to attach it to the pole. Large, plain metal curtain rings would also work well.

1 Tape the canvas to the wall. Mark the dimensions of the final hanging, leaving a border to be neatened at the end. Apply two coats of the base colour. When dry, fix the stencil plate in the top centre of the canvas and roll on the second colour.

2 The small motifs at the bottom of the plate provide the register for the next move, in this case to one side. Move the plate, aligning it on the register marks, and work as above.

3 When the top band of the pattern is complete, move down the canvas, registering the plate on the stencilled pattern above. Allow to dry. Trim the edges with a sharp knife against a straight edge.

Tip

Stage 2 shows that the stencil plate is a 'negative' of the final pattern, i.e. paint is applied to the spaces between the motifs, rather than the motifs themselves. If the plate had been cut as a 'positive' of the pattern, it would be very frail and difficult to use. See page 26.

INDIAN
PAISLEY
MOTIFS

Faded sepia pictures of Victorian forebears wearing solar topis and ladies in white muslin frocks and cartwheel hats gathered for tea on screened verandas conjure up images of India which are much exploited today in fashion photo-shoots and films. The combination of richly timbered interiors, beds draped with mosquito netting and elaborately worked metals and woods are now familiar motifs. The projects here have all the romance of a bygone era, but are remarkably easy to re-create.

A delicate lace stencil in a golden ochre provides a wallcovering which is luxurious, romantic and remarkably easy to create.

1 Paint the frame with the base colour and allow to dry. Mark the centre of each side of the frame and lay a strip of masking tape so that it butts up to the centre point on the outside of the area to be worked.

2 Tape the stencil plate to the frame, aligning its outside edge on the outer edge of the frame. Stipple on the second colour. Mask the centres of the remaining sides, then stipple paint through the plate to the opposite corner of the frame.

PICTURE FRAME WITH A
BOLD BORDER

This simple picture frame is decorated with the bold design that is also used for the door surround on page 88. Repeating motifs on small items, such as lampshades or picture frames, is an ideal way to create a sense of unity in a scheme, and gives any room a considered, designer look. This design is particularly strong so it should be used with care. Here, a striking combination of black on ochre adds to the effect; for a more subtle image you could use two closely related tones: for example, a greenish-blue on blue or two shades of green, picking the colours from the picture in the frame.

The stencil plate is the one used for the border corner on the door surround. Mirror images are created by flopping the plate. After working one corner, the plate is turned over for the next, pivoting it on the centre point so that the pattern is symmetrical. It is then turned over again for the next corner, and so on.

In practice, it is easier to paint opposite corners first because they use the same side of the stencil plate. The plate can then be cleaned before turning it over to work the last two corners.

First, find the centre of each side of the frame, and mark it in pencil. Lay a strip of masking tape so that it butts up to the centre point on the outside of the area you are going to be working – this ensures that the pattern finishes neatly at this point and gives you a central symmetry. Paint one corner, then the one opposite. Clean the stencil plate and allow it to dry. Remove the strips of masking tape and lay down new ones, again on the outside of the areas to be worked. Paint the remaining two corners using the reverse side of the stencil plate.

This project illustrates the flexibility of the stencilling technique and the way in which a single stencil plate can be used for many different applications.

3 Wash the paint off the stencil plate and allow it to dry. Remove the masking tape and re-apply it on the outside of the centre point, over the already-stencilled areas. Now stencil the last two corners using the other side of the stencil plate.

When the paint is dry remove the masking tape. Finish with two coats of matt polyurethane varnish.

DOOR WITH A
DECORATIVE BORDER

This border picks up on the love of enrichment which is a feature of much folk and ethnic art. The pattern is dramatic and elaborate and is used to give importance to an otherwise plain door. It could be used equally well around a window or an archway.

This stencil plate is the same as that used on the picture frame on page 86. The effect, however, looks very different. The frame was painted black on a pale ground, while here the pattern is picked out in white on a black background so that it is read in reverse. This illustrates very well the way an image changes when you reverse the tonal emphasis, using a light colour instead of a dark one and vice versa. These changes play tricks with our perception and can render a familiar pattern almost unrecognizable. If you use colours which are close in tone, so that there is less contrast between one area and another, the pattern becomes less obvious. Sometimes you want a pattern to

You Will Need

●

Stencil plate 1: border corner, from template p.141
Stencil plate 2: border, from template p.141
Emulsion paint in 2 colours: one for the background, the other for the motif
Medium decorating brush
Medium stippling brush
Palette
Masking tape
Ruler
Pencil

●

catch the eye and 'read', while at others you want it to sit quietly in the background. Here, a bold effect has been achieved by using highly contrasting colours so that the border stands out against the subtle, lace-effect wall pattern.

As with the picture frame, the 'mirror' technique is used, this time when applying the border plate, to make the border symmetrical about the centre of the door. First, stencil the border corner. Then measure the width of the border above the door and mark the centre. Lay a strip of masking tape down the centre point on the outside of the area to be worked. Stencil the border up to that point, then lift the stencil plate, move the masking tape to cover the other side of the centre point and replace the stencil plate, positioning it so that the motif 'mirrors' the pattern already painted. There is no need to turn the stencil plate over, as was necessary for the frame, since the border plate is symmetrical.

2 Mask the centre of the border above the door. Register plate 2 on the corner motif and stipple the border, making it symmetrical as described above. Then, again registering on the corner, apply the vertical band.

1 Using the background colour, paint a band, the width of the border, around the door. (Use masking tape to define the border edges.) Tape stencil plate 1 in position and apply the second colour with the stippling brush.

Tip
In any location where symmetry is essential, 'mirror' the stencil plate around the centre point. Mask the centre point and turn the plate over, so that one side of the image 'mirrors' the other.

3 Registering the plate on previously stencilled areas, work round the door until the border is complete. For a neat architectural finish, apply a strip of moulding that has been painted to match the door.

LACE-PATTERNED WALL AND CUSHION

This stencil effect is easy and very effective – and you don't even have to cut a stencil. You will need a piece of lace with an all-over pattern. Choose one that suits the style and period of your decorative scheme. Here, the lace has a traditional Kashmiri teardrop motif.

To use lace as a stencil, it should be stretched on a frame. When buying the fabric, look for the repeat in the pattern and make sure the width of the fabric gives you at least two repeats so that you have something to register on. Similarly, buy a long enough length to give you more than one repeat, and allow for some overlap to attach the lace to the frame or stretcher. Make the frame from four lengths of timber or from artist's stretchers. The frame should be large enough to give you more than one pattern repeat to the side and to the top. It is essential that the frame is square. To check this measure the diagonals – they should be the same length.

You Will Need

●

Piece of lace
Frame to stretch the lace
Staple gun or tacks and a hammer
Aerosol of paint, a spray gun or a Humbrol Power Pack
Emulsion paint for the walls, thinned 1part paint: 1 part water
Fabric paint for the cushion
Gold fabric paint (optional)

●

It is important that the lace is placed straight in relation to the frame, otherwise it will be impossible to align the repeats correctly when stencilling. Lay the fabric on a flat surface – iron it first if necessary – and place the frame over it so that the pattern is straight. Attach the fabric to the frame using a staple gun or tacks. To minimize distortion, fix the centre of one side, then the centre of the side opposite and then the centres of the remaining two sides. Then work from the centre to the corners, working on alternate sides.

The lace should be taut but not overstretched, otherwise it will tear or the frame and the pattern will become distorted.

Since the frame prevents you from stencilling into the corners of the room, fill the edges with a border, such as the one around the door, once the main area is decorated. For a co-ordinated effect, the lace pattern can also be used with fabric paint on a cushion, as here.

1 To make the lace stencil, lay the lace flat and place the frame on it, making sure the weave of the lace is square to the frame. Fold the lace over the frame and attach it to the back with staples or tacks (see above).

2 Using the lace stencil plate is a two-handed job, so ask someone to hold it in place on the wall while you spray on the colour. Use a compressor and spray gun if you have access to one; alternatively, use an aerosol paint. Cover adjacent areas to protect them from the paint mist.

1 Lay the fabric for the cushion on a clean surface and tape it in place, masking off a border if required. Mix the fabric paint with some gold fabric paint (optional) and fill the spray gun.

2 Spray on the paint, then fix it by ironing. To protect the surface, lay a sheet of clean paper over the painted fabric before you begin. (Note that the lace stencil is yellow because it was used for the wall decoration.)

Tip
Always wear a mask when using spray paint in any form. Disposable masks and masks with replaceable filters can be bought from all decorating and DIY stores. They are cheap and absolutely essential.

3 Remove the masking tape to reveal a neat, clean edge. Stencilling fabrics is a useful way of creating soft furnishings which co-ordinate with the decorative scheme. Stencilling works best on smooth fabrics like plain cotton.

MOROCCAN TILE PATTERNS

Islam has given rise to a very particular style of ornament which has been applied in all the decorative arts. Much of Islamic art is characterized by an absence of any kind of naturalistic or figurative representation, and almost all of it tends towards flat abstract patterns and stylization. The result is an art rich in strong colour and pattern. Some motifs recur time and again, in both ceramics and textiles. The complex intertwining lines of the arabesque which is the basis of the wall tiles on the next page are believed to have evolved from a stylization of natural forms like vine leaves and the acanthus.

*Tiles in glorious colours
create a sumptuous and exotic
setting. But these 'tiles' are
not what they seem — they
have been stencilled using a
fascinating technique.*

MOROCCAN
TILED WALL

Ceramic tiles are popular because they are tough, resistant to water, staining and heat, and are easily wiped clean. They are also highly decorative. They may be glazed or unglazed, patterned or plain, and vary in shape, size and thickness. You can choose from period, regional or contemporary styles. Some are very cheap; others, and probably the ones you've set your heart on, are hand-made or antique and can be very costly. Here, a completely convincing tile effect has been created by mixing texture compound with paint. If you are prepared to spend a little time cutting the stencils and preparing the mixes you can cover your walls with the rarest and most costly looking 'tiles' at a fraction of the price of the real thing.

This project and that on page 98 re-create geometric tile designs reproduced in the catalogues of an exhibition on Moroccan ceramics. The colour scheme is authentic:

intense blue and sunshine yellow set off by white and given emphasis by black. You could achieve a very different effect by changing the colours or applying the design on a different scale. Or you could use it as a flat pattern without the texture compound.

With all practical tasks it pays to plan ahead and stencilling is no exception. If you look at the main stencil you will see that around the outside edge of the stencil plate the motifs are incomplete. In many of the other projects in the book (for example, the *All-Over Wall Pattern*, page 70) whole motifs are used as the register for the repeats, both up and down and sideways. Here the stencil plate is cut so that it is possible to get a register for the repeats by slotting the plate 'up to', rather than on top of, the previous motif. In this way the wet mix is not disturbed.

Stencil plates 1, 2 and 3 should follow the same route across the wall, so it might be useful to draw yourself a rough map of the moves.

You Will Need

●

Stencil plate 1 from template p.142. Stencil plate 2 from template p.143. Stencil plate 3 from template p.143
Trowel or plasterer's small tool
Emulsion paint in 4 colours: blue, yellow, white, black
Texture compound
4 mixing pots and sticks
Masking tape
Sandpaper
Varnish and wool roller
Chalk line, filling knife, sponge

●

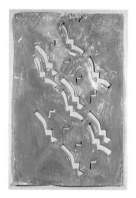

1 You will need three stencils to create this design – stencil 1 for the blue, yellow and black motifs, stencils 2 and 3 for the white. Mix the texture compound with each of the emulsion paints – the mixture should be stiff enough to form peaks.

2 Establish a vertical in the centre of the wall using a chalk line. Fix plate 1 on the chalk-line at the top of the wall. If all the plates follow the same route the process will be much more accurate.

Tip
Two plates are needed for the white pattern as one would be too weak – from Stage 9 it can be seen that the ties which hold the lattice together are very frail. Bear this in mind if you are cutting your own motif.

3 Trowel on the paint/
texture-compound
mixture. Apply all three
main colours – blue,
yellow and black –
through the plate in turn.
(You may find it helpful to
have a coloured-in chart
to hand, to show where
each colour should go.)

4 Lift off plate 1.
Working down the
wall, reposition plate 1
using one of the motifs as a
register. Then go back to
the top of the wall and
work down again, butting
the stencil up to the
completed panel to the side.
Apply plate 1 to all the walls
before moving to plate 2.
When dry (after about 12
hours), rub down with
sandpaper (see Stage 8).

5 Position plate 2 so that the register mark apertures butt up against the side of the yellow motif.

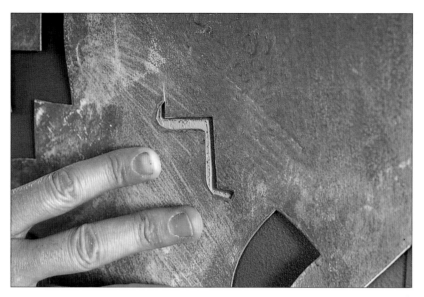

6 Apply the white paint/texture-compound mix through the plate, levelling off the top with the trowel. Continue until the walls are covered. When dry, rub down with sandpaper.

7 The wall with stencils 1 and 2 applied. Now position plate 3, registering it as above. Apply the white paint/texture-compound mix through the plate, as in Stage 6. When complete, leave the walls to dry and then rub down with sandpaper.

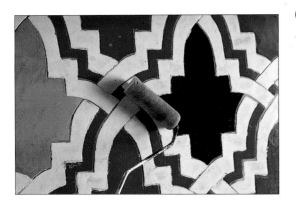

8 The surface should be sandpapered after each stage to remove any ridges that might interfere with the laying in of the next application of paint/texture-compound mix.

10 Mix texture compound for the 'grout' and apply to the spaces between the 'tiles' with a filling knife. Work over a large area – the texture compound won't dry out too quickly – then use a wet sponge to wash off the surplus.

9 Apply four coats of polyurethane varnish for a high-gloss 'fired' finish. Use a wool roller to give a smooth surface without brushmarks.

ANTIQUE TILE
EFFECT

In this project paint is again mixed with texture compound to create a relief effect which looks and feels remarkably like wall tiles. As with the previous project the geometric motif is taken from Islamic art, but here it is given a contemporary twist by using a restrained palette of black, white and oatmeal and 'distressing' the surface.

A simple border at top and bottom gives the tiled area a neat finish. Decide how high you want the main tiled area to go, and how deep the border should be. Mask the top and bottom of the 'tiled' area with tape, allowing space at the bottom of the area for the border.

The three colours are applied separately, and the paint/texture-compound mix must be left to dry thoroughly between applications – about 12 hours depending on the drying conditions. The best plan is to do one stage each day, leaving the surface to dry overnight. When the first

You Will Need

●

Stencil plates 1: all-over pattern from template p.144. 2: all-over pattern from template p.144. 3: border from template p.145. 4: border from template p.145
Emulsion paint: white, black, 'light stone'
Texture-compound mix
Plasterer's small tool
Wool roller and polyurethane gloss varnish
Sandpaper: aluminium oxide 60 grade, masking tape

●

application is dry sandpaper it lightly to remove rough edges; this makes it easier to apply the second stencil.

When the black and white have been applied through the main stencils and the pair of border stencils, and when the entire surface is completely dry, give it a light sanding before applying two coats of polyurethane gloss varnish. Allow 12 hours drying time between each coat. The varnish gives the tiles a gloss finish – it also acts as a barrier between the paint/texture-compound mix and the 'grout'. The grout is actually texture compound mixed with 'light stone' emulsion paint to look like bleached plaster. It is applied over the entire surface with a filling tool and left to dry. At this stage the surface looks messy but sanding the 'tiled' area vigorously cleans the grout from the surface. It also creates the appearance of very old tiles. Compare this with the brightly coloured tiles in the dado on page 92.

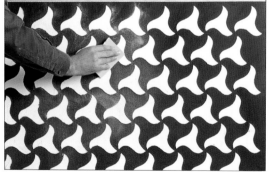

1 Mask the top and bottom of the area to be tiled. Fix stencil plate 1 to the wall and apply white paint mixed with texture compound (see page 45) using a plasterer's small tool. Lift the stencil carefully. For the repeat, slot the stencil over the previously worked section.

2 When the first colour is dry (approximately 12 hours) sand the surface lightly to remove sharp edges which would catch on the second stencil.

3 Apply stencil plate 2. The registers are triangles cut in the stencil. They align with the edge of the white area so that a gap is left between the black and white motifs. This gap is important because it allows for the 'grouting' between the tiles.

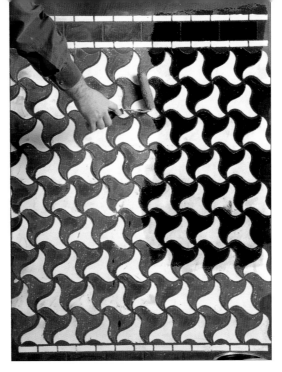

7 Sand the entire 'tiled' surface and then apply two coats of polyurethane gloss varnish using the wool roller. Allow 12 hours for each coat to dry.

4 Apply black paint/ texture-compound mix through stencil 2 using the plasterer's small tool. Remove the stencil carefully and repeat, following the same route as you did for stencil 1. Continue until the entire area has been covered. Leave to dry and then remove the masking tape at the top.

5 Now do the border. Apply stencil 3 by aligning it along the top of the 'tiled area', but shift the plate up slightly to allow a gap for the 'grout'. Apply white paint/texture-compound mix with the plasterer's tool. Remove the stencil and repeat using the motif as the register.

8 The 'grout' is a mix of 1 part 'light stone' emulsion paint with 2 parts texture compound. To this you should add a little water to create a creamy, easily workable consistency. The mixture is applied over the entire surface using a filling tool. Make sure it is worked into the gaps between the tiles. Leave to dry.

6 Leave the white to dry, sand lightly and then apply stencil plate 4. The register triangles are designed to align with the corners of the white areas.

9 When the 'grout' is dry (about 12 hours) the entire surface is sanded vigorously to give the tiled surface an aged and distressed appearance.

10 Here you can see that the edges of the tiles are broken here and there, while the glossy film of varnish has been roughened or entirely removed in places. Use the aluminium oxide sandpaper (or a rotary electric sander if you have one). Wear a mask as the process creates a lot of dust.

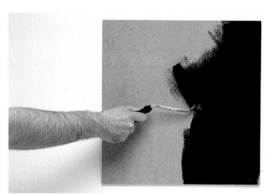

1 Apply black under-coat to the tiles with the wool roller. Allow to dry. Then apply the black eggshell. Allow to dry.

Tip
When designing your own tile patterns, consider 'spreading' the complete design over four tiles so that the overall effect is not too dense.

2 Position the stencil plate over the tile so that the border butts up to all the tile edges. Fix the plate in place using holes cut in its centre. Apply white paint to the entire pattern with the sponge gloss roller.

3 When the white paint is dry, stipple on each of the three remaining colours in turn. Have a chart to hand to show which colour goes where, and use a guard to protect adjacent areas.

FLOOR TILES WITH A *DIAMOND* AND *TRIANGLE MOTIF*

This tiled floor uses a repeating pattern of diamonds and rectangles. To see the complete pattern, several tiles have to be looked at together, as each tile carries only half of the motif (see Stage 5). This is an important consideration when you are planning your own stencils. If you had put the entire pattern on the stencil plate, the design would have built up very differently: each tile would have had the complete border so that laid together the pattern would have been duplicated, creating a much denser design.

This project shows you a simple, cheap, effective and remarkably enjoyable way of making your own floor tiles. They are made from medium-density fibreboard (MDF) and are a good way of covering up a poor quality wooden floor or concrete. Sheets of MDF were cut down to 45cm (17 3/4 inch) squares, which makes the work much easier: you can stencil a few tiles at a time and work comfortably at a table, rather

You Will Need

•

Stencil 1 from template p.145
Black oil paint: undercoat and
eggshell. Emulsion paint in 4
colours: white, blue, green,
terracotta
Wool roller for black paint, gloss
sponge roller for white paint. 3
small mottlers for the blue,
green and terracotta
Palette, masking tape and guard
Fine wet-and-dry sandpaper
(silicon carbide)
Varnish, MDF (see below)

•

than having to bend over a large sheet on the floor.

The tiles are decorated using one stencil plate, through which are applied a base colour and four detail colours. You can use the same colours as here, or select shades to suit your particular colour scheme. Whatever you do, planning is important. Start by making a trace of the stencil on a piece of lining paper and colour it in so that you know where the five colours are to go. Have this to hand as you work.

From the picture opposite, it can be seen that the paint surface is slightly broken, which gives the tiles a worn, handmade appearance that is easy on the eye and looks authentic. The finished tiles were protected with a polyurethane varnish. If you think your colours look too garish, you can knock them back by tinting the varnish with a touch of raw umber artists' oil colour. Then simply fix the tiles to the floor using tile adhesive.

4 Wet the sandpaper and rub back the colours to create a 'distressed' effect. Then apply three coats of polyurethane varnish to give a hard-wearing surface.

5 Four tiles laid together show how the complete pattern builds up.

MODERN INSPIRATION FROM ANCIENT EGYPT

The civilization of ancient Egypt has had a strong hold over the European imagination from the very earliest times. From the Egyptians we have taken a host of decorative motifs which are so much a part of our visual world that we often don't see them or don't recognize them for what they are; for instance: the lotus column, the sphinx, the lion's paw, the palmette leaf, cross-legged chairs with leather seats, mother-of-pearl inlays and various veneering techniques. Here, motifs from that ancient world are re-created, so that their authenticity is retained, but with a highly contemporary twist.

The world of antiquity has been plundered for the profusion of patterns in this striking living room, while the delicious colour comes from modern Barcelona.

DOOR PANELS WITH A
SILHOUETTE BORDER

Doors are a significant, though often overlooked, feature of any room – in many rooms there is more than one door so that they account for a large part of the wall space. It is surprising, therefore, that in many beautifully decorated and furnished rooms, on which a considerable amount of time and creative effort has been lavished, the doors simply don't fit into the decorative scheme.

Here, bright yellow paint and stencilled panels add interest to a rather boring flush door. A stencilled border describes the panels and links the door with the decorative scheme. Three colours are used: black for the background and bright green and rich terracotta for the details.

Two stencil plates are needed: the first for the background; the second for the details. Plate 1 is a silhouette of, and slightly larger than, plate 2. Plate 1 is applied first, producing a black silhouette of the motif. The details are

You Will Need

●

Stencil plate 1: silhouette, from template p.147
Stencil plate 2: details, from template p.147
Emulsion paint in 3 colours: black, green, terracotta
Medium stippling brush for the base colour
2 small stippling brushes for the details
Palette
Masking tape, Post-it notes
Guard

●

then applied through plate 2, which is removed to reveal a neat, black border. This method underlies almost all the designs shown here, and you may find it useful when designing your own stencils.

It is important to plan the divisions of the door carefully – you can do this by eye or take the proportions from another door. Here, the top panel equals the combined area of the lower two panels, so the division is not arbitrary. Spend some time experimenting. When you've established the rectangles that you find most satisfying, draw them on the door using soft pencil or chalk. Once these dimensions are established, you can grid up the template to give you the stencil plate at the most appropriate size. Make notes about moves and where the colours are to go so that you have something to refer to as you work. The more time you spend planning, the more smoothly the stencilling process will go. The panels have been trimmed with a narrow beading.

1 Fix stencil plate 1 in position with masking tape. Put Post-it notes or masking tape under the register mark apertures to provide the alignment for plate 2. Stipple on the black, making sure that you apply colour to the register marks.

3 Here, the silhouette is complete; the register marks have been left in place for the alignment of the second stencil plate.

4 Position plate 2, aligning it on the register marks. Stipple on the green and then the terracotta, using a guard if necessary to protect previously painted areas. Work round the panel until complete.

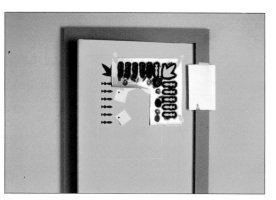

2 Work the opposite corner, again placing Post-it notes or masking tape under the register mark apertures. Stipple on the black paint as above. Continue until you have completed the panel in the first colour.

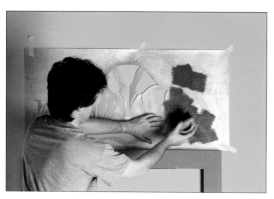

2 Position plate 2, aligning it using the register marks (see introduction, opposite). Apply each of the remaining four colours in turn, using the large picture, above, as a guide.

1 Centre stencil plate 1 over the door and fix in position with masking tape. Stipple on the base colour (brown), remembering to hold the plate firmly against the wall to prevent paint seeping underneath it.

Tip
Experiment with different colourways on scrap paper before you apply a stencil to a wall or door. Cut out the painted motif, tape it in position and leave it there for a few days to see if it works. If not, try again with different colours.

3 Here, the black is being applied. Work with care and hold the plate flush to the wall so that paint does not seep underneath it and spoil the fine details.

DOOR PEDIMENT WITH A
STYLIZED FLORAL MOTIF

In decoration it is the details that tell, so attention to those finishing touches can make the difference between a result which is satisfactory and one which is completely convincing. Here, a decorated architrave 'finishes off' a doorway.

Architraves were originally introduced to disguise a joint in the plasterwork, or the junction between one material and another. They used to be made from stone, plaster or wood, and were substantial and beautifully moulded. Nowadays the surround to a doorway is often no more than a thin strip of wood. The appearance of a room can be considerably improved by adding a decorative or more substantial architrave to openings.

Here, a large stylized floral motif was used to give a flourish to a doorway. The style and colourways have been selected to tie in with the rest of the room scheme and in particular with the panels on the door. The motif could have many applications in a home. Use it, for example,

over an otherwise plain window or over the opening between two rooms. Or you could combine it with the border from the door to make a frame for a plain mirror on a chimney breast.

Since it is big, bold and symmetrical, this motif can stand alone, but it could be also be repeated to provide a pediment for a wide opening. If you apply it in this way, use an odd number of repeats, three or five, as asymmetry is more satisfying than an even number of motifs. As with the stencil for the door panel on page 107, there are two stencil plates. The first provides the base/silhouette motif and is larger than the second. In this case, dark brown is used for the base colour. It is less harsh than the black, and works better at this larger scale. The registers are a series of nicks cut into the plate (see the templates on page 147). These registers allow you to align on the outer edge of the 'silhouette motif'.

4 Here, the final colour is applied. A guard is used to protect areas which have already been painted. This motif is not difficult; it simply needs planning and care when painted. And, as can be seen from the illustration opposite, the effect is stunning.

DADO WITH A
ZIG-ZAG MOTIF

In the decorative scheme of a room the dado usually occupies the lower metre or so of the wall, defined by the skirting at the bottom and a moulding or rail at the top. The dado was usually treated in a different way from the rest of the wall because it was liable to be knocked by passers-by and by furniture. In traditional houses this part of the wall was often panelled, tiled or gloss painted, while the upper part was covered in wallpaper, which was an expensive commodity. The height of the dado rail conforms to the height of a chair back because, before the late eighteenth century, chairs were normally ranged around the edge of the room.

It was in the early eighteenth century that the tripartite division of the wall into frieze, field and dado was first introduced. Originally, the proportions were derived from the architrave, column and base of the classical orders. Before that time wood panelling usually extended from floor to ceiling. The relative proportions of the dado and frieze have fluctuated as fashions changed.

Here, a bold zig-zag pattern makes an ideal decoration for an existing dado; alternatively, it could be used to provide a division of the wall where none exists. Dramatic but simple, it is ideal for hallways and would also enliven any bathroom.

The pattern requires two stencil plates. It is a good example of a pattern which would have fragile ties if it were cut on a single plate (see page 26). If the pattern was cut on a single stencil plate, the yellow zig-zags, which are the background showing through, would be the ties and the plate would be frail and floppy, making it difficult to use.

It is important to cut this stencil carefully and to ensure that you cut the register marks accurately. A simple geometric design like this is less forgiving than many apparently more complex designs.

You Will Need

•

Stencil plate 1 from template
p.148
Stencil plate 2 from template
p.148
Emulsion paint in 2 colours:
burgundy and green
2 large stippling brushes
Palette
Masking tape
Chalk line

•

1 Draw a horizontal chalk line to mark the top of the dado. Starting at one end of the wall, fix stencil plate 1 in position with masking tape and stipple on the first colour, burgundy.

Tip
To establish a horizontal you need a vertical. Use a chalk line to find a vertical at the midpoint of the wall. Working from this point use a spirit level to create a level horizontal line. This is better than measuring up from a floor which may slope.

2 Work along the top of the area, using the painted pattern as a register. Then move down, again registering on the painted pattern. Continue in this way until the first colour is complete.

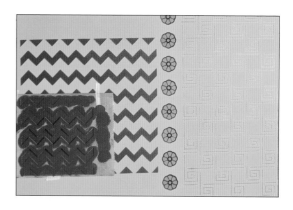

3 Position plate 2, using the register marks to align it. When correctly aligned, the undecorated wall will be visible through the plate, but the burgundy will be completely covered. Stipple on the second colour as in Stage 2.

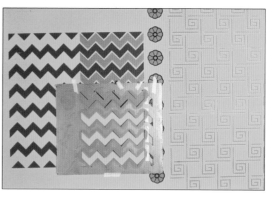

111

COLOURWAYS

Violet and lilac applied through the zig-zag stencil plate used on pages 110–111 create a cool, harmonious look for a hallway. Violets also work well with their parent colours, cool crimson reds and warm blues; in addition, exhilarating colour schemes can be created by combining violet with shades of yellow. Here, the plain upper wall and the chair's bold design give the pattern a contemporary feel.

GREEK KEY
PATTERN

The Greek key pattern, also called the classical fret or meander, is traditional, ubiquitous, and has a great many applications. Its construction is interesting; it is basically a continuous interlace of straight lines with a repeating right angle. Examples can be found all over the world in different cultures including the Egyptian. It has been carved, painted and woven on to every surface imaginable. It can be seen as a carved relief border in the twelfth-century Cluniac church of Saint Croix at La Charite-sûr-Loire, on Indian pottery from South America, textiles from Peru and incorporated in a thirteenth-century wall in Mexico. It was popular in Europe during the neo-classical revival of the eighteenth century and from that time on it has been painted, carved or inlaid on furniture and floors, painted on walls, printed on wallpapers and incorporated in painted or encaustic tiles. Here it has been used as an all-over design, but it

You Will Need

•

Stencil plate 1: vertical lines,
from template p.149
Stencil plate 2: horizontal lines,
from template p.149
Emulsion paint in 1 colour
Small stippling brush
Palette
Masking tape

•

could be applied equally well as a border.

The pattern cannot be cut on a single stencil plate because it is a continuous line and there are no natural ties to link the centre of the motif with the outside. Instead, two plates were cut: one with the vertical lines; the other with the horizontals. A small diamond is cut into plate 1 to mark the top edge. As with the zig-zag pattern on the previous pages, accurate drawing and cutting are important.

Once the plates have been cut, practise painting up the design on lining paper. After you have painted the verticals through plate 1, lay plate 2 over the painted area – starting in the same location. The horizontal lines on plate 2 must butt up to the vertical lines to give you the pattern. Stage 2 shows that when this happens the vertical lines are completely hidden by the second plate. This basic construction could be adapted to create a border – a popular use of the Greek key motif.

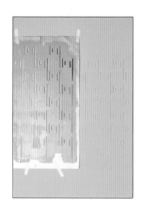

1 Position plate 1, making sure the edge with the cut diamond is at the top of the area to be painted. Stipple on the paint, then move the plate, registering it on the painted area. Continue until the whole area is covered.

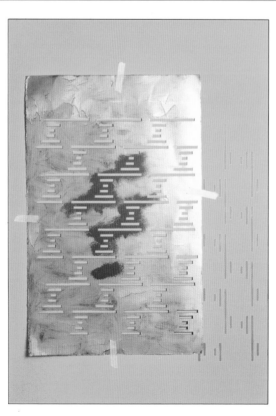

2 Position plate 2 over plate 1. The pattern provides its own register: plate 2 is correctly located when none of the painted vertical lines can be seen through the horizontal cuts. Stipple on the paint as in Stage 1.

3 Here, the relationship between the vertical and horizontal lines, and the way the pattern builds up, can be clearly seen.

 COLOURWAYS

Deciding what colours to use in a decoration is a subjective matter; however, some combinations are more suited to certain applications than others. Here, black on a brick-red background is evocative of traditional floor tiles and therefore feels appropriate. Care must be taken with an all-over geometric pattern like the Greek key, as strong colour contrasts can often create optical vibrations which are distracting and tiring on the eye. So always experiment with different combinations of colour before you finally commit yourself.

FRIEZE WITH A *FLORAL MOTIF* AND *TOOTHED BORDER*

The frieze is the part of the traditional tripartite division of the wall, below the cornice and above the picture rail. The term is also used to describe a painted or sculpted motif.

The depth of the frieze varies depending on factors such as the period of the house, the height of the ceiling in relation to the size of the room and the effect you want to create. In Arts and Crafts houses, for example, the frieze was often very deep.

There are many reasons why you might want to introduce a frieze into a room. It is a useful way of visually modifying the proportions – horizontal elements like dados and picture rails reduce the apparent height of a room by interrupting the vertical space. Like the dado, a frieze can be used to create more satisfactory proportions in a tall room or in a narrow corridor.

A frieze, together with other architectural details like a dado and cornice, can be used to give a period flavour to

You Will Need

●

Stencil plates 1: background to floral motif, from template p.150. 2: details of floral motif, from template p.150. 3: background to border, from template p.151. 4: details of border, from template p.151
Emulsion paint: brown, black, orange, green, blue
Medium stippling brush and 4 small stippling brushes
Palette, masking tape, guard

●

an otherwise featureless room. But it is important to think about the proportions. Many modern homes have rather low ceilings and too many horizontal divisions of the wall can be oppressive, because they appear to bring the ceiling down.

This frieze consists of two main components: the stylized floral motif and the toothed border below it. Each of these requires two stencil plates: one for the dark, single-colour background; the other for the details. The process resembles that used to create the panel on the door on page 107 and the design above it (page 108).

There are two ways to establish the working line for the frieze. One is to draw a horizontal line by measuring down from the ceiling, marking off points at regular intervals and joining them up to give a base line. An easier method is to make sure the stencil has a regular border which will butt up against the ceiling and ensure that the stencil is always the same distance from it.

2 Position plate 2 so that the register apertures – tiny nicks cut into the plate at the base of the design – butt up to the brown background. Stipple each of the four remaining colours in turn with the small brushes, using the illustration opposite as a guide.

1 Starting in the centre of the wall, position plate 1, aligning it on the baseline or against the ceiling (see introduction). Working from the centre of each wall outwards, stipple on the base colour with the medium stippling brush, using the painted motifs as a register for the repeats.

Tip

Instead of bending the plate into the corners, stop the frieze short and paint in a vertical line or rectangle. It is easier, and reduces the risk of damaging the plate. See 'Using a Stop', page 41.

3 Here, the fourth colour is being applied. With a plate of such fine detail, use a guard to protect the previously painted areas.

4 Work plates 3 and 4
in the same way,
butting them up against
the painted pattern. Apply
the brown base colour
through plate 3 using a
small stippler; then stipple
three colours in turn
through plate 4.

FRENCH EMPIRE STYLE

T he Empire style dates from the years after the French Revolution. Colourful, frivolous and fun, it also managed to be refined and restrained. While it took its name from the first empire of Napoleon (1804-14), it lasted into the 1830s, and its influence spread far beyond the borders of France. The designs and decorations shown here were inspired by an Empire wallpaper found in an old pattern book; the daring colour combinations and the exciting stencilled effects and textures capture the grandeur and richness of the period.

Stencils and colour have been used with verve to create an extravaganza of colour, pattern and texture in this opulent Empire-style drawing room.

Wall with a
Rope Stripe

Colour can have a dramatic effect on our mood and on the way we perceive things. You can use colour to make a cold room feel warmer, a small room bigger, an austere room feel more inviting. Here, a glorious Schiaparelli shocking pink is held in check by a simple rope stripe. A gleaming gold star at the base of each stripe provides interest on the dado border and acts as a visual link with the gilded furnishings.

A stencilled stripe is a very simple way of decorating a plain wall. Start by deciding how widely spaced the stripes should be – this will depend on the proportions of the room, the colours of the stripe and the background, and whether the decorated wall will be hung with pictures and mirrors. Closely spaced stripes tend to emphasize the height of the room while widely spaced ones make the ceiling feel lower. The stripes here have been applied at 50cm (19 1/2 inch) intervals.

You Will Need

•

Stencil plates 1, 2 and 3 from the templates on page 152; stencil plate from template on page 152 for the gold star
Emulsion paint: black, brown, green
Medium stippling brush and 2 mottling brushes
Palette, masking tape, tape measure and chalk line
Plasterer's small tool
Gold powder; Liquitex medium sand texture

•

Planning is important. Start from the most important corner of the room – the one you see as you enter – and make the stripe work at that junction. Here they are arranged symmetrically around the corner.

The rope stripe uses three stencil plates. First, plate 1 is fixed in position and black paint stippled through it. From this stripe, a 50cm (19 1/2 inch) gap is measured to locate the next one. The positions of all the stripes are measured from the first one. Once completed, the black stripes act as 'maps' for stencil plates 2 and 3.

When you draw up stencil plate 2 from the template, start by tracing in the outline of plate 1. This allows you to position register mark apertures – nicks cut to butt up to the edges of the painted motif when plate 2 is correctly located – in the second plate. Similarly, when drawing up plate 3, first trace in the outline of stencil plate 2 to give you a location for the register marks.

2 Work round the room, spacing the stripes evenly. Then position plate 2, aligning the register apertures in the plate against the edge of the black stripe. Stipple on the second colour (brown) with a mottling brush.

1 Locate the position of the first stripe using a chalk line. Centre plate 1 on the line and stipple on the base colour (black). Work down the wall, aligning the plate on the painted pattern and keeping it centred on the chalk line.

3 Align plate 3 on plate 2, using the cut register apertures to ensure the plate is correctly positioned. Stipple on the final colour as in Stage 2, working down the stripe and aligning the plate on the painted pattern.

1 Establish the horizontal baseline for the border using a plumb line and a spirit level. Mask off the required depth with masking tape and paint it black. Mix texture paste and gold powder on the palette.

Tip
Acrylic mediums like the one used here dry quickly. Spraying the mix with water from a plant sprayer will help to keep it moist and workable.

2 Position the stencil plate by aligning it under the rope stripe. Tape the plate to the wall and trowel on the gold powder/texture paste mix, then level it off. Peel the stencil plate off carefully and reposition for the next motif.

1 Align the edge of the stencil plate with one edge of the tile and fix in position with masking tape. Apply black paint, making sure the roller is not overloaded and that you apply even pressure.

FLOOR TILES WITH A
STAR AND BORDER

This floor design is simple but effective and would enhance any hallway or living area. As with the Moroccan tiled floor on page 102, panels of medium-density fibreboard (MDF) cut to 45cm (17 1/2 inch) squares were used. Here, the squares were painted with a 'grain' to simulate rosewood. However, the pattern would work equally well on a plain ground. Almost any colour combination will work with such a simple design. Black on cream or red would have a bold, contemporary feel, while two shades of the same colour, such as dark blue on light blue or holly green on sage green, would look more traditional and subdued. Once again, it is worth cutting the stencil plate and experimenting. Start with 'safe' combinations which relate to the existing decorative scheme. But also take the opportunity to explore more challenging ones. An unconventional use of colour can give an otherwise restrained scheme a real lift.

You Will Need

●

Stencil plate from template
p.153
Black emulsion paint
Gloss sponge roller
Palette
Masking tape
Polyurethane varnish
MDF panels cut to 45cm (17 1/2 inch) squares

●

To create this pattern you need only one stencil plate. As explained in the section on ties (see page 26), a plate of the complete square border cannot be cut as the middle section would fall out. Instead, the plate comprises just two sides of the border. It is positioned on the MDF tile and held with masking tape. Paint is then applied to the star and to the border areas. Because the star is non-directional, the plate can then be turned and re-applied to the tile so that the missing two sides of the border can be stencilled, thus completing the continuous line.

In the Moroccan tile pattern on page 102 the plate overlapped the tile. Here the pattern is within the tile area so the stencil is smaller than the tile. By cutting the stencil so that it fits the area exactly you can align the edge of the stencil plate on the edge of the tile. Tape the plate in position by taking the masking tape over the edge and on to the back.

2 The motif after the first move. Replace the plate so that the border slits fall on the sides of the tile which have no border. The edges of the tile and the painted star motif provide the register. Roll on black paint as in Stage 1.

3 Remove the stencil plate to reveal the tile with a continuous border. Apply at least three coats of polyurethane varnish for a hard-wearing surface. Allow the varnish to dry completely between each application.

STONE-EFFECT
DADO

A rugged, *faux* stone-effect dado provides a surprising contrast to the elegance of the rope border and the sumptuously gilded furniture. Marble and stone effects are a useful way to introduce varied textures and surfaces into a room scheme. Sometimes the intention is to deceive the eye by faithfully reproducing naturally occurring marbles, but often fantasy or *faux* marbles are created solely for their decorative quality. When exploring these techniques it is important to consider the way in which they will be seen and to find an approach which is appropriate. For example, while a dado in a large room will be viewed in passing and from a distance, a small box will be picked up and scrutinized and will need to be painted in a more detailed way.

The method for creating a relief surface which captures accurately the texture of a stone wall is similar to that used for the Moroccan tiled wall (page 95). Texture com-

You Will Need

•

Stencil plate from template
p.153
Texture compound
Emulsion paint in 4 colours: a
stone colour (green), and 3
shades for the mottling
Trowel or plasterer's small tool
Wool roller
Pot and stick for mixing
Palette
Matt polyurethane varnish
Masking tape

•

pound is mixed with paint and applied through the stencil plate.

When the surface is completely dry the stencil plate is re-applied and random colour painted on with a roller to suggest the tonal variations that are found in natural stone or marble. The secret of this technique is to select your colours carefully but to apply them in a manner which is bold and free. Here, the base colour is green, with three related shades used to achieve a natural, mottled effect. All three colours are laid out on the palette. They are then loaded on to the wool roller. A random effect is achieved by working the roller over the 'stone' surface briskly with frequent changes of direction (see page 37).

This technique has many applications. While the green stone effect shown on page 120 contributes to the opulence of the setting, the mellow tones used for the bathroom, opposite, have a more rustic 'country' appeal.

1 Mix the texture compound with the green paint until it is easily workable but stiff enough to hold its shape. Fix the plate in position and trowel on the mixture. Remove the plate and work the next section.

2 Repeat the process, working along the dado area until it is complete. Leave to dry.

3 Put some of each of the 'mottling colours' on the palette and work the roller through them so that they are all picked up. Roll the paints over the surface, constantly changing direction in order to create a random blending of colours.

4 When dry re-apply the stencil plate and seal the surface with three coats of varnish. The varnish protects the surface, gives the colours great depth and intensity and suggests the hard, shiny appearance of natural stone.

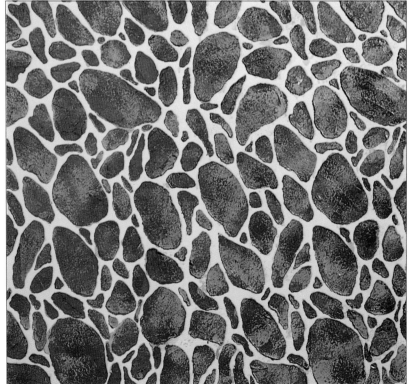

A FLORAL
SCREEN

This luxuriant design is based on a pattern from a book on French wall-papers dated 1800-50. The project is complex and challenging and illustrates the possibilities of the stencilling technique. The result is so detailed that at first glance it looks painted. The pattern builds up using 11 stencil plates and 11 colours, including four shades of yellow, four shades of pink, and black, yellow and brown.

The most difficult and time-consuming part of the process is drawing the templates and then cutting the stencils, but if you are naturally meticulous and methodical, and if you enjoy working in a precise way – making patchwork quilts or cabinet-making, for example – you will relish the challenge.

Accurate registration is important if the design is to come together accurately. You must ensure that each template and stencil plate relates correctly to the previous one in the series. The best way of checking this is to trace down

You Will Need

•

Stencil plates 1-11 from
templates pp.154-7
Emulsion paint in 11 colours: 4
yellows, 4 pinks, black, brown
and green
Medium stippling brushes
Small stippling brushes
Mottling brushes
Palette
Masking tape
Matt polyurethane varnish
Pencil

•

the outline of the previous stage first, and fit the next one within it. Sometimes it is useful to trace the outline of several stages using different colours to identify them. The register marks must be located outside the pattern area and drawn with great accuracy on each stencil. Identify each template and stencil carefully as you work. On this project the numbers 1 to 11 are cut into the stencil plates – this is also a handy way of checking which is the right side. If you place the numbers in the same location you will also be able to tell at a glance which is the top and which is the bottom.

When you do the project keep the build-up picture close to hand for constant reference – you will find it an invaluable aid. For example, if you look at number 9 in the build-up overleaf you will see that the stencil plate has been designed so that the black paint goes over the outer edges of the blossoms. In this way the 'negative', the background, is used to give them a neat edge.

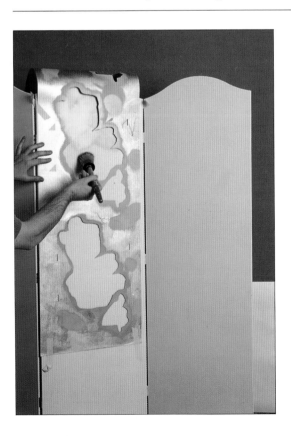

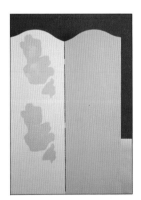

1 The complete sequence of the build-up is shown overleaf. Here, plate 1 is in place. In pencil, draw the register marks on to the screen. They are very important because they provide the key for the next 10 stencils.

2 Here, colour 1 creates the broad forms of the blossoms.

3 Plate 5 is in position. It has been applied using the triangular registers to get the correct alignment. Colour 5 is the first of the pinks – see overleaf – and establishes the centres of the flowers.

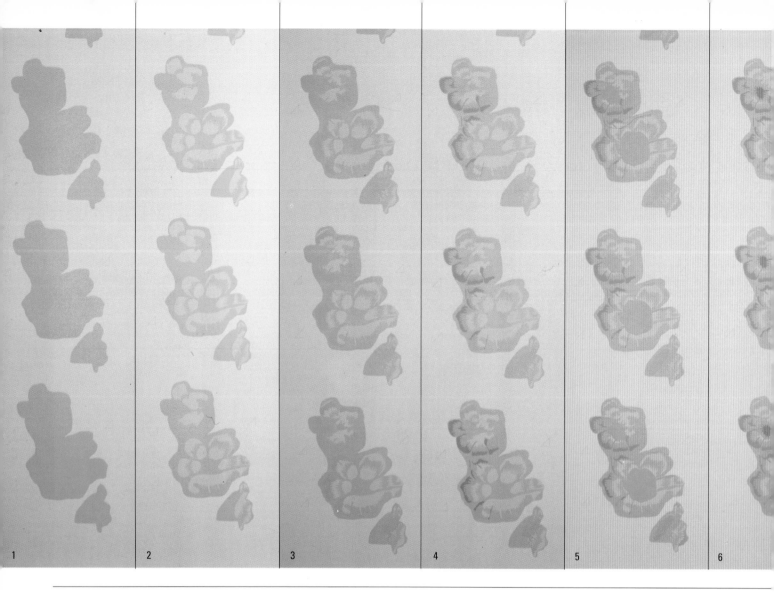

1   2   3   4   5   6

4   The pattern is beginning to build up, the yellows defining the tonal variations on the flowers and the pink describing the flush in the centre of the blooms.

5   Plate 9 is in position. Black applied through this plate provides the background for the leaves between the flowerheads. The stencil has been cut so that the black paint goes over the outer edges of the blossoms and gives them a neat edge.

6   This picture corresponds to stencil plate 10, above: the brown paint which gives the broad forms of the leaves has been applied through the plate.

7

8

9

10

11

7 The final plate in position. It carries the details of the leaves. For intricate work like this, use a small stippling brush.

8 The final pattern has many of the painterly qualities of a freehand painting. There is a great deal of naturalistic detail in the leaves and in the blooms which you would not normally expect to find in a stylized pattern.

Tip

The registers for this project are diamonds which are cut into each stencil plate – they can be seen in the illustrations, at various points beyond the outer margins of the stripe. In previous projects we have suggested you painted the register marks on to Post-it notes. Because of the complexity of this project it may take a long time and Post-it notes are likely to fall off before you are finished. More permanent register marks can be drawn in pencil directly on to the surface. When you are finished the marks can be rubbed off or painted out.

TEMPLATES AND STENCILS

The templates and/or stencils for all the projects in this book (with the exception of the lace stencil for the projects on pages 84 and 85) are illustrated on the following pages. Use the templates to create your own stencils. The simplest, single motif designs, can be traced, gridded up or enlarged on a photocopier. A stencil can then be cut following the instructions on pages 28—33. In other instances the template has to be mirrored and repeated to create the stencil plate. The stencil plates used in the step-by-step demonstrations have been reproduced as a guide.

Repeats. For any pattern which repeats, the stencil plate must incorporate a register for the repeat moves of the stencil plate. The simplest example of this is the pineapple stripe (project on page 52, stencils and template on page 133). The stencil plate includes two pineapple motifs, one to drop over the painted motif to provide the register and one to be painted. Border designs must also include enough motifs to provide a register. All-over patterns like the Pugin wall pattern (project page 70, stencils and template page 137) and the wall hanging (project page 82, stencils and templates page 140) must have enough repeats to allow you to register both horizontally and vertically.

Registers for multi-plate designs. Where a design consists of more than one plate it is important to be able to register successive plates accurately. There are three main systems of registering.

Sometimes the pattern provides its own register. The zig-zag dado design (project page 110, stencils and templates page 148)

and the Greek key pattern (project page 114, stencils and templates page 149) are good examples of this.

In the second system, nicks cut in a stencil plate register on an element of the design that was painted with the first stencil plate. The rope stripe design (project page 122, stencils and templates page 152) is an example of this. Nicks in plates 2 and 3 register on the 'background' painted through stencil plate 1.

The final system involves cutting register marks in all the stencil plates. These are placed beyond the area of the painted pattern. The first register mark is drawn on to the surface being decorated and provides the key for all the succeeding stencil plates. The mark is removed or painted over when the stencilling process is completed. If you want to protect the surface the register marks may be drawn or painted on to pieces of masking tape or Post-it notes which are removed when the project is complete.

Where register marks are necessary they have been drawn on to the templates on the following pages. For clarity they have been printed in red.

Stencils and brushes can be ordered from
Tony Roche Stencil Design. For an order form write to:
PO Box 4915, London, SE16 1UQ.

Border stencil page 38

(1) This stencil is used to illustrate all the basic stencilling processes in *Basic Techniques*, page 24.
(2) To draw the stencil the template is mirrored. The foliate motifs at either side of the plate are completed using the template. You need two to provide a register for repeats, see page 30.

A pineapple striped wall, page 52

(1) Cut the stencil plate to the exact width of the stripe for vertical alignment. The stencil plate can then be butted up to the edge of the stripe.

Cupboard with a simple leaf motif, page 48

Bread pot with a three-colour leaf motif, page 50

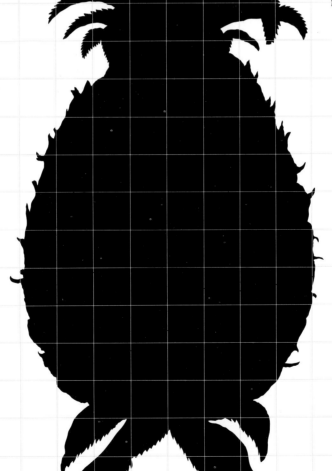

Cabinet with a wood inlay
effect, page 56

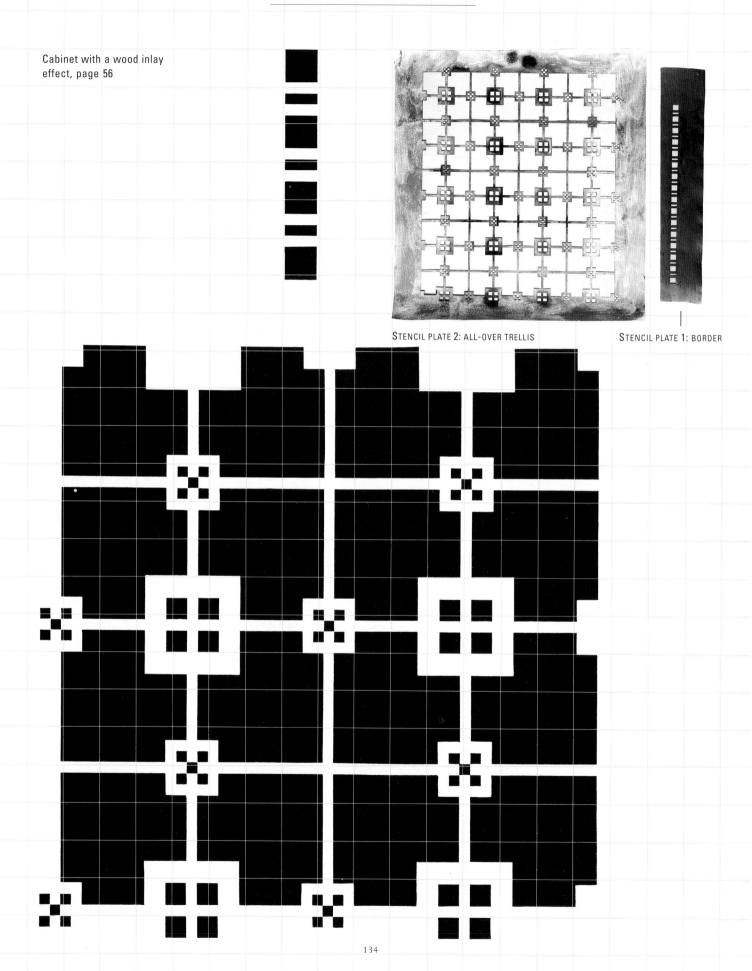

STENCIL PLATE 2: ALL-OVER TRELLIS

STENCIL PLATE 1: BORDER

An Art Deco floorcloth,
page 60

Heraldic tray, page 68

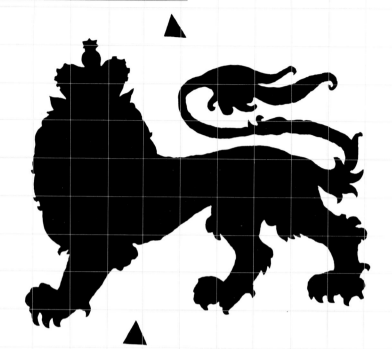

STENCIL PLATE 1:
SILHOUETTE OF LION

STENCIL PLATE 2:
DETAILS OF LION

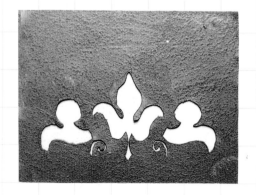

Lampshade with a border motif, page 66

All-over wall pattern, page 70

(1) The template motif interlocks to create the repeats, see stencil.

(2) The stencil plate used for the project had 13 repeats but five will give you enough repeats to register vertically and horizontally.

(3) Cut a separate motif to fill gaps, see page 72.

Fireplace with a textured
motif, page 76

STENCIL PLATE 1: FLORAL MOTIF

STENCIL PLATE 2: FLEUR-DE-LIS

Box decorated in gold, coral
and blue, page 78

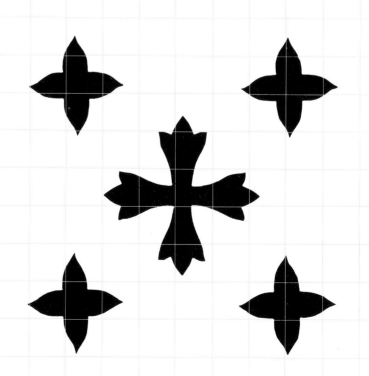

STENCIL PLATE 4: MAIN MOTIF

Floor with a geometric tile design, page 80

(1) You need four triangles to make up a square stencil. The stencil used for the demonstration had six triangles to provide convenient registers for the repeats.

(2) The 90-degree angle border can be 270 degrees depending on which side you cut the border. The space between the motif and the edge of the stencil dictates the distance from the wall and this must be consistent.

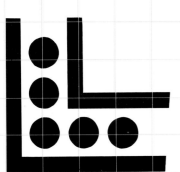

STENCIL PLATE 2: 90-DEGREE CORNER

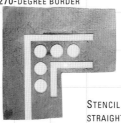

STENCIL PLATE 3: 270-DEGREE BORDER

STENCIL PLATE 1: STRAIGHT BORDER

Wall hanging with a heraldic motif, page 82

The pattern on this stencil is large. If there were several complete repeats the plate would be too big and flimsy. To overcome this the plate incorporates only enough of each repeat to provide a register. Compare the template with the stencil plate to see exactly how it has been constructed. First the template is mirrored to the right to give the width of the plate. It is then moved down and certain elements of the pattern are drawn to provide a vertical register. The centres of four floral shapes are completed to provide registers for sideways moves.

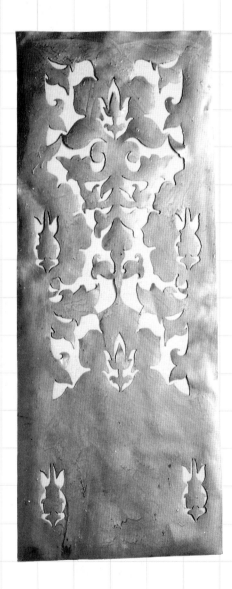

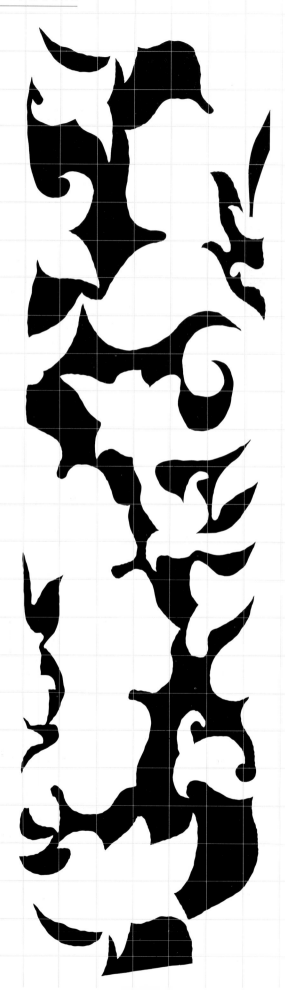

Picture frame with a bold
border, page 86

(Stencil plate 1 only)

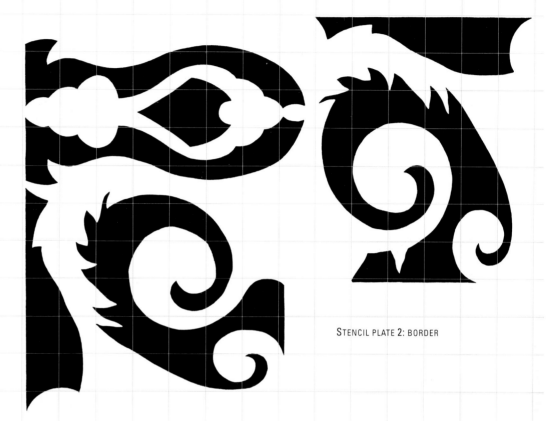

STENCIL PLATE 2: BORDER

Door with a decorative border,
page 88

Stencil plate 1: border corner
Stencil plate 2: border

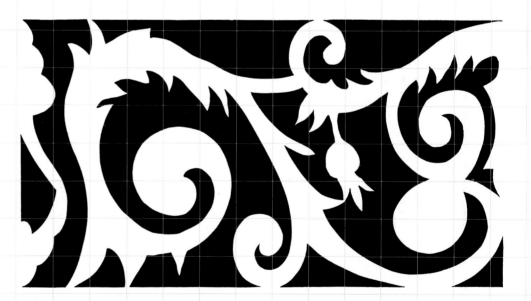

STENCIL PLATE 1:
BORDER CORNER

MOROCCAN TILE PATTERNS

**Moroccan tiled wall,
page 94**

(1) The painted pattern from stencil 1 will provide the register for stencil plates 2 and 3 (the white trellis).

(2) Note that stencil plate 1 is cut with 'open' motifs on the edges. The stencil plate can be butted 'up to' the painted area for repeats. This avoids dropping it over the painted area and disturbing the wet texture/paint mix.

(3) If the stencil plates are to be used with a texture compound they should be given two coats of cellulose paint for extra protection.

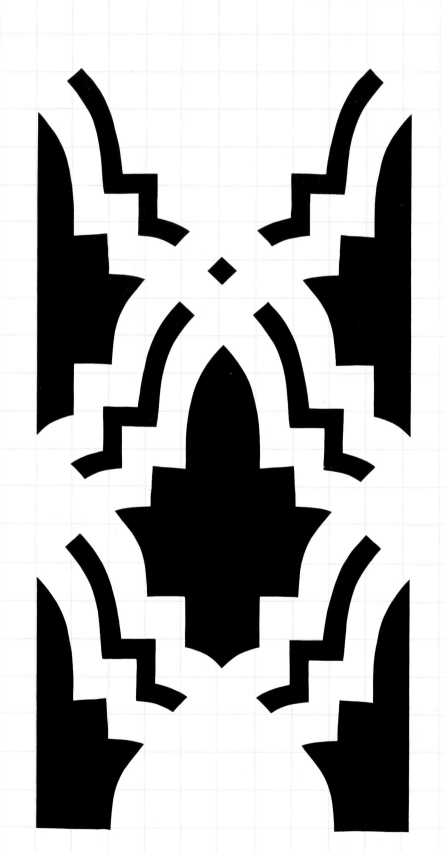

STENCIL PLATE 1

STENCIL PLATE 2

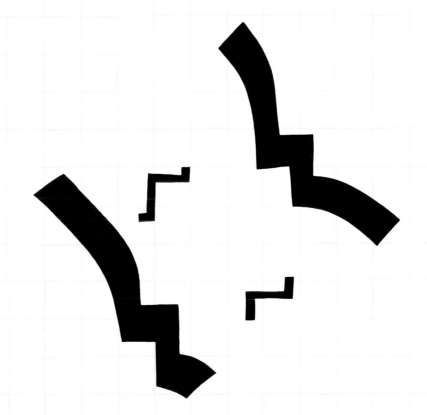

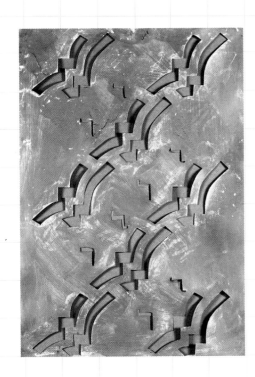

STENCIL PLATE 3

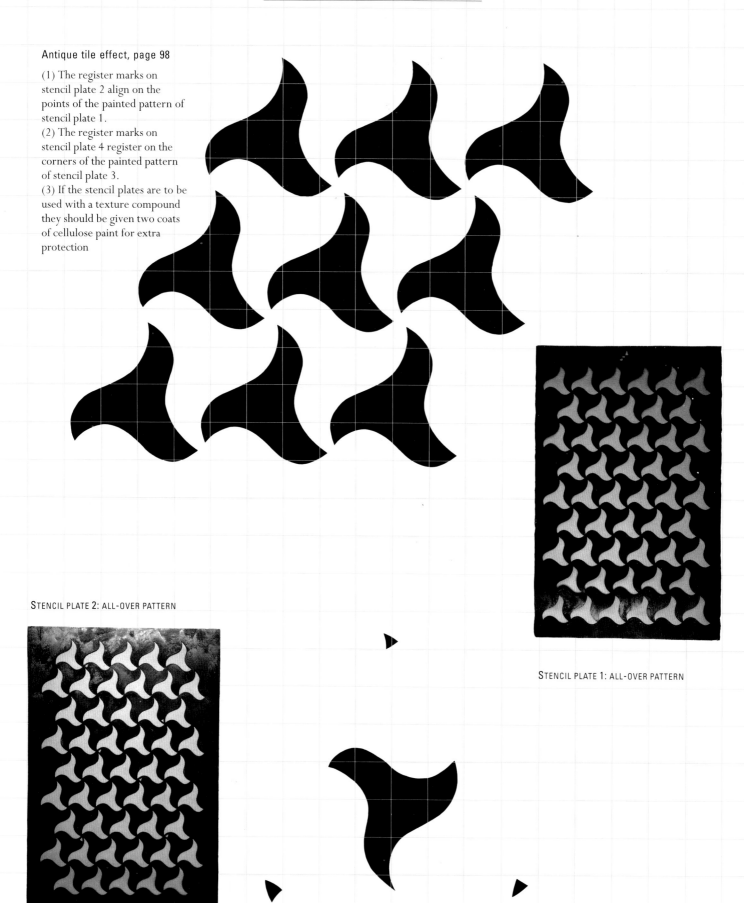

Antique tile effect, page 98

(1) The register marks on stencil plate 2 align on the points of the painted pattern of stencil plate 1.

(2) The register marks on stencil plate 4 register on the corners of the painted pattern of stencil plate 3.

(3) If the stencil plates are to be used with a texture compound they should be given two coats of cellulose paint for extra protection

STENCIL PLATE 2: ALL-OVER PATTERN

STENCIL PLATE 1: ALL-OVER PATTERN

Floor tiles with a diamond and
triangle motif, page 102

(1) The template design allows you to
construct your own corners.
(2) Because the pattern butts right up to
the edge of the tile the stencil plate
overlaps the edges of the tile. The
triangles cut in the middle of the stencil
plate allow you to fix it to the tile.

STENCIL PLATE 4: BORDER

STENCIL PLATE 3: BORDER

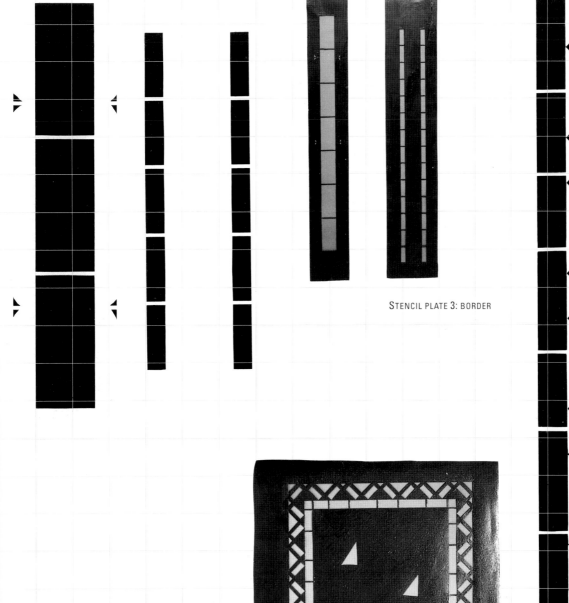

Door pediment with a stylized
floral motif, page 108

(1) Template is mirrored to give
the stencil design.
(2) Nicks must be cut in
stencil plate 2 so that it can be
registered on the background
design.

Door panels with a silhouette
border, page 106

STENCIL PLATE 2: DETAILS

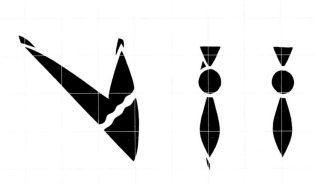

STENCIL PLATE 1: SILHOUETTE

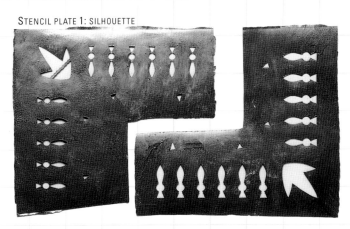

STENCIL PLATE 2: DETAILS

Dado with zig-zag motif
page 110

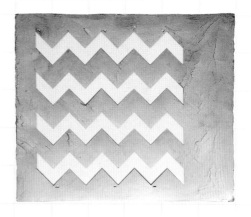

Greek key pattern, page 114

Stencil plate 2 registers on the painted pattern from stencil plate 1. Stencil plate 2 is designed to be slightly oversize to allow for this.

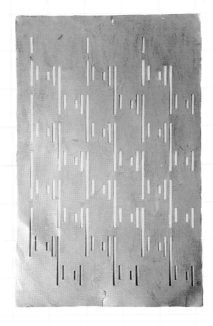

STENCIL PLATE 1: VERTICAL LINES

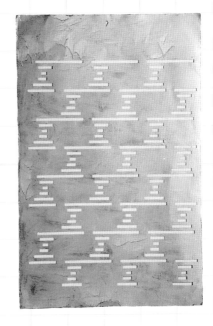

STENCIL PLATE 2: HORIZONTAL LINES

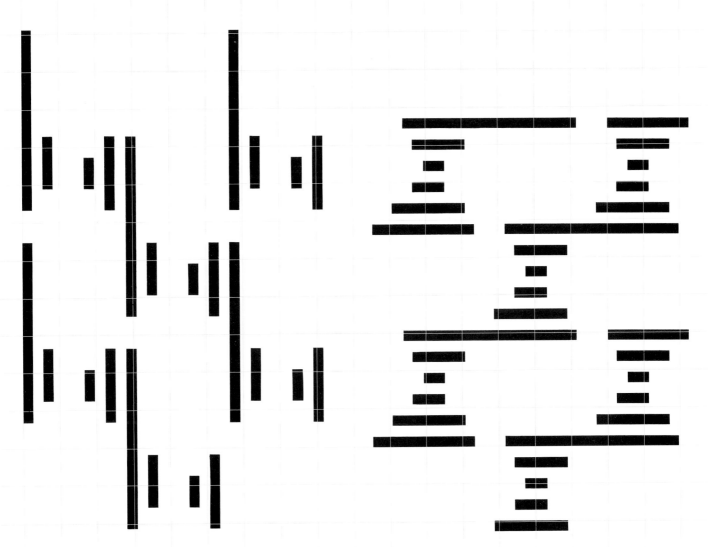

Frieze with a floral motif and toothed border, page 118

Cut nicks in stencil 2 so that it can be registered on the painted design from stencil 1.

STENCIL PLATE 1: BACKGROUND TO FLORAL MOTIF

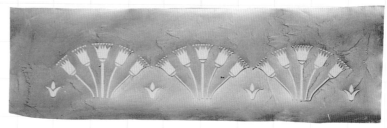

STENCIL PLATE 2: DETAILS OF FLORAL MOTIF

Border for Greek key, page 114

This was not step-by-stepped.

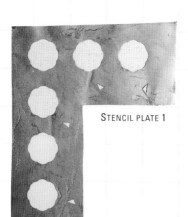

STENCIL PLATE 1

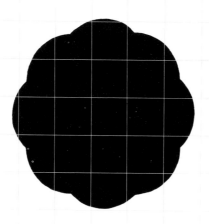

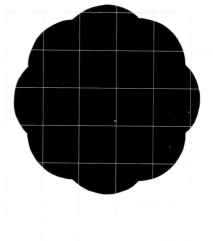

STENCIL PLATE 2

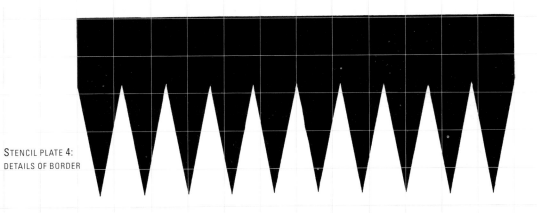

STENCIL PLATE 3:
BACKGROUND TO
BORDER

STENCIL PLATE 4:
DETAILS OF BORDER

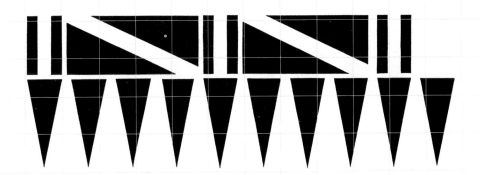

Wall with a rope stripe,
page 122

Cut nicks in stencil plates 2 and
3. These register on the outline
of the background, painted
through stencil plate 1.

STENCIL PLATE 3

STENCIL PLATE 1

STENCIL PLATE 2

Gold star, page125

152

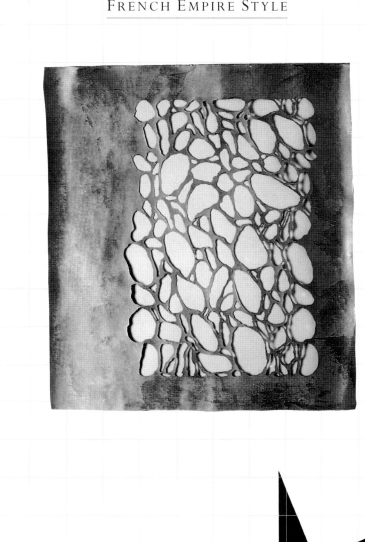

Stone-effect dado, page 126

The template consists of a single row of stones which repeats on both ends of the stencil plate. This provides a register for the moves of the plate. Fill the area between with stones drawn freehand.

Floor tiles with a star and border, page 124

(1) The template is mirrored to create the stencil.
(2) Cut the stencil plate to the exact size of the tile. The edge of the tile can then be used as register.

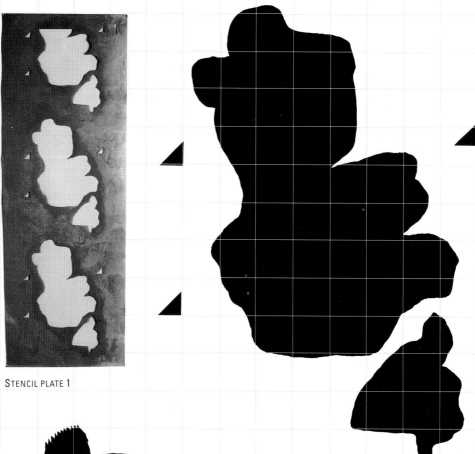

STENCIL PLATE 1

A floral screen, page 128

(1) Register marks must appear outside the pattern area.

(2) Register marks must be cut in to each stencil.

(3) Number each template and stencil, and cut the number into the stencil plate for easy reference.

(4) The template for stencil plate 9 has more register marks that the other tmeplatesbecause it aligns differently in order to create the background between the flowers.

STENCIL PLATE 2

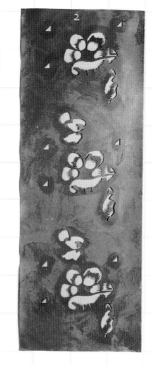

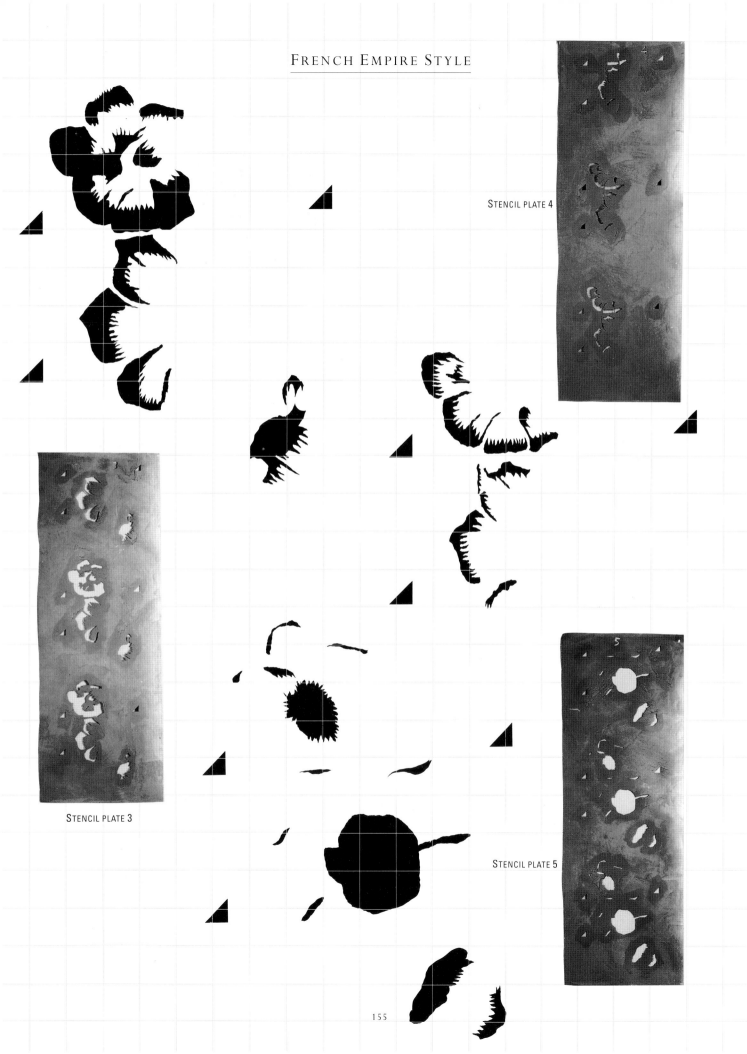

STENCIL PLATE 4

STENCIL PLATE 3

STENCIL PLATE 5

STENCIL PLATE 7

STENCIL PLATE 6

STENCIL PLATE 8

STENCIL PLATE 9

STENCIL PLATE 11

STENCIL PLATE 10

SUPPLIERS

Where to find brushes, paints, paper, and other fine art supplies.

Art Essentials of New York, Ltd
3 Cross Street
Suffern, NY 01901-4601
(914) 368 1100

Art Supply Warehouse
360 Main Avenue
Norwalk, CT 06851
(203) 849 1112

Daniel Smith Inc.
4150 1st Avenue South
Seattle, WA 98134
(800) 426 6740

Gail Covisi Stenciling Inc.
405 Haddon Avenue
Haddonfield, NJ 08033
(800) 338 1325

Hirshfield's Decorating Centers
725 Second Avenue North
Minneapolis, MN 55405
(612) 377 3910

Janovic Plaza Inc
30–35 Thomson Avenue
Long Island City, NY 11101
(800) 777 4381

Loew Cornell Inc
363 Chestnut Avenue
Teaneck, NJ 07666
(201) 836 7070

New York Central Art Supply
62 Third Avenue
New York, NY 10003
(212) 473 7705

Pearl Paint
308 Canal Street
New York, NY 10013
(212) 431 7932

Purdy Corporation
13201 N. Lombard
Portland, OR 97203
(503) 286 9217

Sid Moses Equipment and Tools
10456 Santa Monica Boulevard
Los Angeles, CA 90025
(310) 475 1111
mail order only

TJ Ronan Paint Corp.
749 E. 135th Street
Bronx, NY 10454
(212) 292 1100

INDEX

INDEX